ALLYSON COOPER

Cricut For Beginners

Your Easy Guide To Know All The Bases About Cricut For Start In The Best Way And Understand Which Is The Perfect Machine Model For You

Copyright © 2020 Allyson Cooper

All rights reserved

© **Copyright 2020 - All rights reserved.**

The content contained within this book may not be reproduced, duplicated or transmitted without direct written permission from the author or the publisher.

Under no circumstances will any blame or legal responsibility be held against the publisher, or author, for any damages, reparation, or monetary loss due to the information contained within this book. Either directly or indirectly.

Legal Notice:

This book is copyright protected. This book is only for personal use. You cannot amend, distribute, sell, use, quote or paraphrase any part, or the content within this book, without the consent of the author or publisher.

Disclaimer Notice:

Please note the information contained within this document is for educational and entertainment purposes only. All effort has been executed to present accurate, up to date, and reliable, complete information. No warranties of any kind are declared or implied. Readers acknowledge that the author is not engaging in the rendering of legal, financial, medical or professional advice. The content within this book has been derived from various sources. Please consult a licensed professional before attempting any techniques outlined in this book.

By reading this document, the reader agrees that under no circumstances is the author responsible for any losses, direct or indirect, which are incurred as a result of the use of information contained within this document, including, but not limited to, — errors, omissions, or inaccuracies.

CRICUT FOR BEGINNERS

Introduction *5*

Chapter 1. Cricut Machine Models *19*

Chapter 2. Cricut Tools And Accessories *35*

Chapter 3. Materials That Can Be Used For Cricut *76*

Chapter 4. Design Space Application *81*

Chapter 5. Cricut Projects For Beginners *104*

Chapter 6. Making Money With Cricut *126*

Conclusion: Tips For Start In The Best Way *132*

Introduction

What is a Cricut?

The Cricut machine is a fantastic creation. This helps you cut paper, cloth, and vinyl sheets to whatever pattern you would like. These actual production designs may be achieved via software tools like the Cricut Layout Studio or via Capsules using pre-engineered structures assembled into them. Therefore, if you're an enthusiastic scrapbooker, this system is a must-have.

What Can I Make With This?

There are several one-of-a-kind problems for you to use a Cricut. While you know what type of task you want to perform, and at the same time considering what kind of decoration and supplies you need to use the machine, please take a look at the rest of the other projects and parts that Cricut has just started. Demand (and what are basically "decent possessions" that you can spend when you need them) Scrapbooking and Card Making.

There are loads of scrapbooking thoughts and scrapbook designs than you can discover for your Cricut!

Or, once you don't want the opportunity to make cards yourself, there are some pointers and special effects for making cards quickly.

Weddings and Gatherings

Cricut machines are great for making custom stylistic themes for weddings and gatherings!

Occasions

Utilize your Cricut to make an occasional stylistic layout for any event!

Home Stylistic Theme

You can make loads of various undertakings to improve your home!

Everything from cushions and divider craftsmanship to big business thoughts!

Clothing and Extras

One of my preferred things to make with my Cricut is shirts, onesies, and tote sacks. You can put warmness switch vinyl on exceptionally much any material surface. However, you can likewise utilize a Cricut to make adornments, headbands, and then some!

Vinyl Decals and Stickers

Our assortment one intrigue is lessening vinyl decals and stickers, and you can do this with the Cricut Maker.

It can cut through any vinyl in no time easily—you should simply make your format in Cricut Design Space, teach the PC to begin cutting; at that point, weed, and change the arrangement to your picked surface.

Texture Cuts

One of the essential selling elements of the Maker is the truth that it comes outfitted with the new product Turn Cutting edge.

On account of uncommon coasting and moving movement—by and large with the gigantic 4kg of power at the back of the Cricut Maker—this ability that the work area can lessen unmistakably any texture.

The truth is out. Denim? Check. Overwhelming canvas? Check. Silk? Check. Chiffon? Check. We've continually constrained using a particular texture shaper sooner, than as the registering gadget lessening machines essentially weren't compelling to deal with more massive textures. We cherish the truth that the Maker is an across the board machine.

It comes furnished with a texture-cutting mat so that you can lessen bunches of textures aside from the utilization of any support. Astonishing!

Sewing Examples

Another key prepared of the Maker is the gigantic Sewing Test Library that you'll get passage to when you've purchased the machine.

It comprises of earnestly many examples—some from Effortlessness and Riley Blake Designs—and capacity you can genuinely pick the model you like, and the Maker will remove it for you.

No additional removing designs physically yourself (and not any more human blunder ruins!)

Additionally, secured is a launder-able texture pen that will call attention to the spot the example parts intend to stable together.

Balsa Wood Cuts

On account of the incredible 4kg of weight and the Blade Sharp Edge (sold independently,) the Cricut Maker can slice using substances up to 2.4 mm thick. That limit thick texture that had before been beyond reach with the Cricut and Outline machines is currently open to us. We can hardly wait to start cutting wooden with it!

Thick Cowhide Cuts

In a similar vein as factor #4, thick cowhide can cut with the Maker!

Natively Constructed Cards

Paper crafters aren't forgotten about with the Maker either.

Paper and card cuts will be less complicated and snappier than at any other time because of the machine's vitality and exactness. Your Scratchpad playing cards just went up a level.

Jigsaw Riddles

We comprehend that the Cricut Maker can cut through significantly thicker substances with the Blade Edge than any time in recent memory.

The central perspective we give it a shot? Making our special jigsaw confound. We'll save you, refreshed!

Christmas Tree Adornments

The Revolving Cutting edge that vows to lessen through any texture is the ideal gadget for designing occasion improvements. Scour the Sewing Design Library for Christmassy designs (we've purchased our eye on the gingerbread man adornment!) lessen out the example utilizing felt, or whatever texture you want, and after that, sew it all in all independently.

Blankets

Cricut has collaborated with Riley Blake Designs to give various sewing designs in the Sewing Design Library.

This capacity, that you can utilize the Maker to remove your sewing correctly, divides before sewing, them aggregately independently.

Felt Dolls and Delicate Toys

One of the Effortlessness designs we have our eye on in the Sewing Design Library is the "Felt Doll and Garments" example. We understand a couple of little women and young men who'd love a natively constructed dish to add to their collections. Just pick the bar, cut, and sew. Simple peasy!

Shirt Moves

You need to arrange the switch in Design Space, load the glow switch vinyl to the manufacturer (or flash it drastically on the HTV if you may feel timid;) it recommends that the PC start cutting, and ironing your switch the shirt. Or, on the other hand, you should utilize the fresh-out-of-the-box new Cricut Easy Press to switch the vinyl—it's everything, the solace of an iron meets the adequacy of a warmness press!

Texture Appliques

Additionally, available to get individually, is the Fortified Texture Sharp Edge in lodging, which will allow you to lessen additional unpredictable material designs, similar to applique.

In contrast to the sharp rotating edge, the Fortified Texture Edge requires reinforced sponsorship on the material to diminish adequately.

Calligraphy Signs

The Cricut Maker's significant selling element is its Versatile Apparatus Framework. It is the element that will verify that you keep up your Maker until the end of time. In reality, it's a gadget machine that exclusively suits every one of the instruments and sharp edges of the Explore family. However, it will fit as a fiddle with every future device and cutting edges made using Cricut.

The vitality of the Cricut Maker limit that you can cut thicker substances than sooner than that is appropriately perfect for intricate gems designs.

And keeping in mind that you aren't in any way, shape, or form, to cut gold, silver, or jewel on there, at whatever point soon, an excellent pair of cowhide rings are just inside reach.

Wedding Solicitations and Spare the Dates

As a whole, we know about how "little" costs like welcomes and sexually transmitted diseases can add to the super price of a wedding.

As makers, we also know how to counter-balance a portion of those costs using making matters like ourselves.

The Cricut Maker is perfect for making staggering welcomes—presently, not exclusively, would you remove confusing paper designs, anyway that calligraphy pen will come in reachable once more.

Wedding Menus, Spot Cards, and Support Labels

You're nearly no longer compelled to creates before the wedding function—you can likewise utilize your Maker to adorn for the gigantic day itself. The sky is just the confinement directly here; however, in all reality, make menus, region playing a card game, and lean toward labels. Attempt, and ensure you utilize a practically identical arrangement for all your stationery to protect the subject upfront.

Shading Book

Do you know these "careful shading" books that are extremely popular at present? And after that, the Maker's total direction is to make your own unique, unquestionably extraordinary, shading book utilizing the Fine-Point Pen device.

Liners

Another part we can hardly wait to make with our new Maker is liners.

The world you claim, as far as substances go—whatever from cowhide to sew, to steel sheets, and everything in the middle.

There are likewise some fabulous liner designs in the Sewing Library to investigate as well.

Texture Key-Rings

Something different that got our attention in the Sewing Test Library was, at one time, a couple of simple designs for fabric key-rings.

Once more, the Maker makes it advantageous—totally decrease out the example, and after that, sew it together.

Headbands and Hair Adornments

Presently, Cricut has propelled a registering gadget that is lessening through thick calfskin; we are fearless thought for mind-boggling, steampunk-motivated hair designs, and even headbands.

Who realized the Maker ought to be so convenient for significant pattern articulations?

Cut-Out Christmas Tree

We know, we know, every individual needs a real Christmas tree eventually of the get-away season. In any case, just on the off chance that you don't have space for a transcending tree in your residence room or, God prohibits, you're hypersensitive to pine, you may need support to make your tree. As the Cricut Maker successfully decreases thick substances like wood, we guess an interlocking wood tree is an incredible task to check with this year. No laser is required when the Maker is available to you no matter what!

How Does It Work?

When you see the finished product from a Cricut machine, you will definitely be blown away. The neatness and appealing look of a typical project done with the Cricut machine will take your breath away. However, only a few people understand the process involved in the creation of such amazing designs.

Curious to know how the Cricut machine is able to cut out materials effectively? There are three major steps involved when using the Cricut machine:

Have a Design

If you have a PC, you can access the Cricut Design Space to access the library of designs. If you have a Mac, you can access the same platform to select a huge variety of designs. In case you don't have any of these two, but possesses an iPhone or iPad, you can use the Design Space for iOS.

If what you have is an Android, you are covered as well. This is because you can take advantage of the Design Space for Android. These are online platforms where you can select any design that best suits your taste.

You can also customize a ready-made design to suit your needs. For example, you can resize it, or modify the shape. You can also add a text or image as you wish, till you have the design just as you want it.

Prepare the Machine

Having selected the design you intend to cut out with the machine, you are ready for the next step. The machine needs to be prepared by turning it on. Once you switch on the machine, you actually don't need to do anything.

You don't have to press any button unless you are using the machine for the first time. In that case, the machine will give you instructions on what to do. It is that simple.

That is why both beginners and experts can make use of the Cricut machine without issues. Your Computer or Phone will have to be paired with the machine via Bluetooth for the first time. However, this will not be needed subsequently because the machine will remember the pairing.

Hence, once the machine is switched on, the pairing between the phone and the machine becomes automatic. The implication of this is that once the machine is switched on, the machine is ready. The next step is to send the design to the machine.

Send the Design to the Machine

This is the last stage of the process of cutting with the Cricut machine. Once the machine is powered on, at the top right corner of the screen, you will see the "Make It" button; this is a big green button on the Cricut Design Space

The first thing the software does is to preview the various mats you have. A mat represents a sheet of material; hence, having two different colors in your project implies two mats. There are times that your project can be a combination of fabric and paper. During such occurrences, you will have a mat representing each material utilized for the project. Once you have prepared the machine, you need to decide the dimension with which the machine will do the cutting. If you intend to make two cards, the machine has to be instructed to make two project copies.

You will find this option at the top left of the Cricut Design Space. Most of the materials you will be cutting will be cut at 12″ × 12″ size. This is because this is the standard size that is the most prominent on the Cricut machine. However, if you prefer a different dimension, you can always alter it. The mirror switch has to be flipped to mirror the design you want in case you want an iron-on design. This has to be done to guarantee that the alteration is reflected by the finished project.

Once you are set to send the design to the Cricut, you will click "Continue." This option can be seen at the bottom right corner of the Cricut Design Space. It is easy to continue at this point because the software will prompt you to take you through what ought to be done.

Don't get what-up about how to set up different projects of different materials and colors. This is because the instructions you need will be displayed on the screen, and you can easily follow through. Once you follow the instructions presented to you by the machine, you are guaranteed top-quality cuttings.

The machine will request that you pick the particular material you want to use for the first mat. Simply choose whether it is paper, vinyl, fabric, leather, or any other material. Once you do this, the machine will automatically adjust pressure, speed, and the brush blade as necessary. Hence, just ensure you do your part of instructing the machine to do your bidding as desired. You can trust the Cricut machine from that point to do all that is needed for a perfect project. After the machine has adjusted itself to cut, you will put the material into the Cricut cutting mat. At this point, you will then load the machine with the mat. What if I am using different materials for my project? That is also not an issue worth disturbing yourself about. This is because the software will take you through how to go about loading different materials. Once you are done loading the machine with the mat containing the material, you are good to go. This is because you will be prompted by the machine, concerning setting the dial cutting, drawing, or scoring.

The machine will proceed to cut out the mat. The pieces that have been cut out can then be gathered by you and used as desired. This is how the Cricut machine works, and it is basically the same principle for every project.

It is obvious that you don't have to be a genius before you are qualified to use the machine. The instructions are simplified such that anyone who can understand basic English language can use it. Therefore, if you have been thinking that you might not be able to operate this machine, you are wrong.

So, go ahead, try Cricut, and begin your crafting journey!

Chapter 1. Cricut Machine Models

Cricut Explore One

Because of its efficiency, it is still being purchased today although this is the oldest present-day Cricut machine and first in the Explore line.

Photo credit: amazon.com

Explore One is ideal for beginners and inexperienced users who want to get into die-cutting, craft cutting, and plotting. The machine isn't advanced like the other Explore models, and it is also the cheapest Cricut machine you can get.

Capability

The machine is also highly capable, even if it's an old model. The system can also handle scoring, and writing smoothly.

Materials

Photo credit: amazon.com

Regardless of the simplicity and the inexpensive nature of the machine, it is still highly capable. You can use this system to cut a range of 60 materials and more. This includes light materials like vinyl and thick materials like felt.

Cutting Force

The machine comes with a top-notch German Carbide Premium Blade, which can cut through light and thick materials alike, cleanly and neatly. Even if Explore One is recommended for beginners, it is very professional. The blade is also highly durable.

As for the cutting width, the Explore One can cut sizes that range from 23 ½" tall and ¼ to 11 ½" wide.

Even though the Explore One seems excellent, there are some activities that you can't do on the Cricut Design Space if you're using this model.

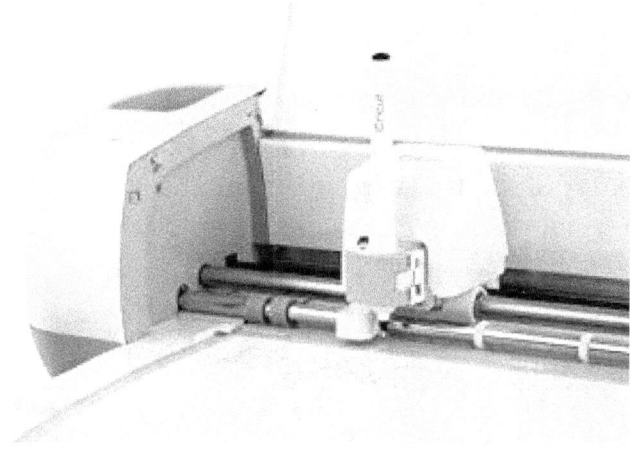

Photo credit: amazon.com

Cricut Design Space is very user friendly when using it for Explore One. It accepts the format files: .jpg, .png, and .bmp.

Also, the Cricut Explore One cannot function wirelessly. If you want to add convenience to it, and you don't mind the cost, then you can buy a Bluetooth adapter and use it to transfer images, or files wirelessly.

The Explore One also comes with one head clamp or carriage only. Because of this, if you want to draw and cut at the same time, you have to buy an adapter.

These are the tools that are in a newly purchased Explore One box:

- 24 x 9.5 x 9.5 sized Cricut Explore One machine.

- German Carbide Premium Blade.

- Over 50 free images.

- Over 25 free one-click projects.

- 12" x 12" Standard Grip cutting mat.

- USB and power cords.

- Vinyl sample.

- Welcome guide.

Cricut Explore Air

Photo credit: amazon.com

While this is quite similar to the Explore One model, it also comes with some additional features. The main difference between them is the presence of the inbuilt Bluetooth adapter. If you don't enjoy seeing cables and wires all around your workplace, especially with the danger of tripping over them, then this model solves that problem.

Capability

The Explore Air is also different from Explore One because it features a double carriage. This means that you can draw, write, or score while you cut because it has two clamps to hold both tools. This saves you money because you don't have to purchase a tool adapter.

Materials

Explore Air is quite liberating when it comes to materials. It features a dial that can allow you to choose the material that you're about to cut. That way, you don't have to guess the blade depth and mess up the material.

The machine will know how deep it will have to cut for felt, and how gentle it has to be for paper or vinyl. This feature is especially great for beginners who are not well versed with the blade depths.

For experienced users, the Cricut Explore Air also features several custom settings that allow the user to customize the cutting of their design.

This model can cut more materials than the Explore One, including fabric, poster board, vellum, and about 70 more.

Cutting Force

Photo credit: businesswire.com

The system is more powerful than the older model when it comes to the cutting force. It features a Cut Smart technology made by Cricut, which enhances the blade control of the system, and gives your creations a more professional look. It can cut anything that is as wide as 23.5 inches accurately and precisely.

It also has the Smart Set Dial, which increases the control you have over the cutting of your project.

The features of the Cricut Design Space are very similar. But, when using Explore Air, you get more freedom, and you are allowed to use .svg, .gif, and .dxf files, in addition to the standard files allowed with Explore One.

Sadly, Explore Air does not have either a knife or a rotary blade. Because of these two types of blades, the Explore Air is recommended for more light crafts and scrapbooking. It does have an inbuilt blade, though.

A brand new Explore Airbox comes with these tools:

- A 25.4 x 10 x 9.2 inches Cricut Explore Air machine with inbuilt Bluetooth technology.
- It has an inbuilt accessory adapter.
- Inbuilt blade.
- USB and power cord.
- Metallic silver marker.
- Iron-on sample.
- Cardstock sample.
- Over 100 images.
- Over 50 ready-to-cut projects.
- 12" x 12" Standard Grip cutting mat.
- Welcome guide.

Cricut Explore Air 2

This is the youngest sibling of the Cricut Explore line. It is the best of the machines in this line. The Explore Air 2, as efficient as the other ones, works even better. It even has a better design, and it comes in different colors than you can do.

Photo credit: amazon.com

Capability

The model features a fast mode that speeds up the cutting process, primarily if you work with deadlines.

It also has the features in the other systems like the German Carbide Premium Blade, inbuilt Bluetooth adapter, dual carriage, and auto-settings.

The great thing about the Explore Air 2 is that it is ideal for both beginners and advanced users.

Materials

This machine can cut through a hundred materials, or even more. This includes, and is not limited to cotton, silk, tissue paper, corkboard, foil, foam, aluminum, leather, clay, chipboard, burlap, and even birch wood.

It also has the Smart Dial, which helps you manage the cutting width depending on the materials.

Cutting Force

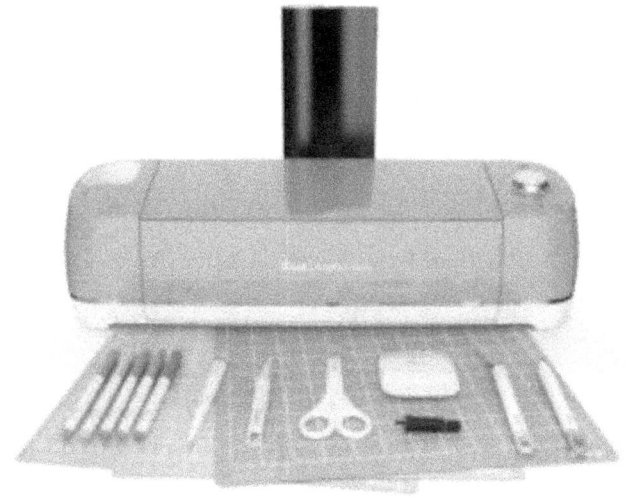

Photo credit: cricut.com

The model is highly potent, and it makes use of the German Carbide Premium Fine-Point Blade, which comes with precision and speed. It is also able to cut any material with a width of 11.5 x 23.5 inches.

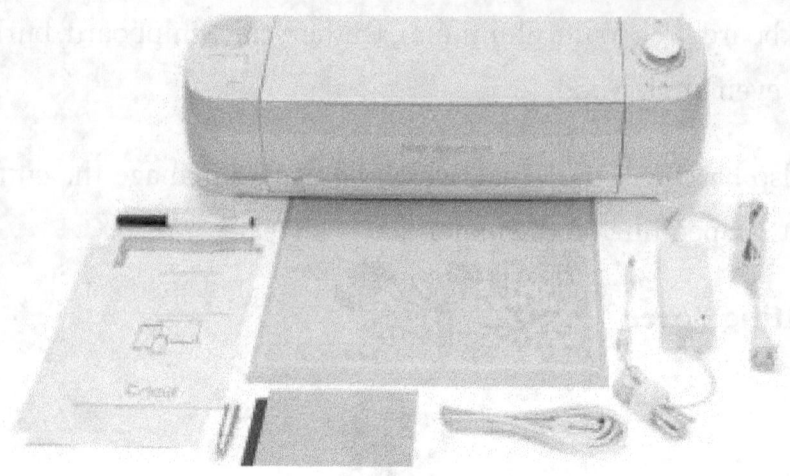

Photo credit: heatbusiness.com

When you first purchase a Cricut Explore Air 2, you get a three months free subscription with access to premium features offered by Cricut.

The Cricut Design Space is also cloud-based for those using iOS devices. With this, you can work offline.

The only downside in this model is the slightly increased noise level, but this is expected because it works two times faster than the previous models.

Your shiny, new Cricut Explore Air 2, will look like this:

- Cricut Explore Air 2 machine.

- Adapter.

- Power and USB cord.

- German Carbide Premium Blade.

- Machine software and application.

- Built-in projects and images.

- Standard Grip cutting mat.

- Cardstock Sample.

- A pen.

- Welcome guide.

Cricut Maker

Photo credit: amazon.com

The newest Cricut die-cutting machine is the Cricut Maker. If you thought that the Explore Air 2 was a great model, then you should get ready to be blown away.

The Cricut Maker is a rare unit amongst other die-cutting machines. The rotary blade is already enough to attract experienced users. And, for beginners, it provides an avenue for improvement and unlimited creativity.

Capability

The Cricut Maker, as an updated version of others, is very powerful and flexible. It comes with a tool kit that includes a rotary-blade, knife blade, deep-cut blade, and fine-point blade. It also comes with a single and a double scoring wheel, as well as a collection of pens. The pens include a fine-point pen, a washable-fabric pen, a calligraphy pen, and a scoring stylus.

Photo credit: amazon.com

The machine also improves its efficiency by adding some unique features. We have the adaptive tool system, which means that the device can adjust the angle of the blade and the pressure of the blade automatically depending on the material. It doesn't need the Smart Dial feature because the Cricut Maker determines your cutting force for you, and its decisions are usually accurate.

It has two clamps, one for the pen or scoring tool, and the other for the cutting blade. This system is also unique because of its fast mode and precise mode. This works for any paper, cardstock, and vinyl.

Materials

As expected, the Cricut Maker will be able to handle more and thicker materials than the machines in the Cricut Explore series.

From light materials to basswood and leather, this machine will exceed your expectations.

Cricut Design Space also provides a lot of benefits for Cricut Maker users. It allows the format files: .jpg, .gif, .png, .svg, .bmp, and .dxf.

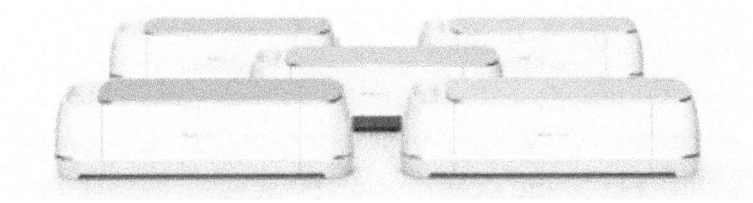

Photo credit: cricut.com

The system also supports a wireless Bluetooth adapter. You can also enjoy the Sewing Pattern Library if you own a Cricut Maker.

The library contains 50 ready-to-cut projects, and it is a result of a partnership between Cricut and Riley Blake Designs.

Another great benefit you get when using Cricut Maker with Design Space is that you get free membership of Cricut Access for a trial period.

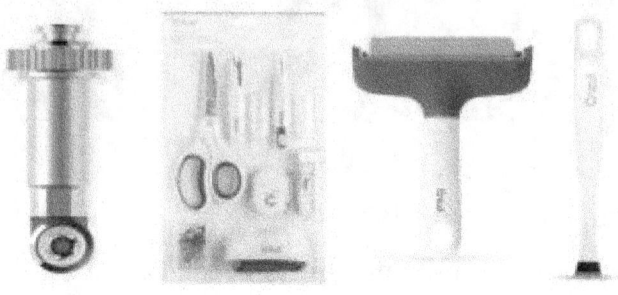

Photo credit: heyletsmakestuff.com

The only downsides to this model are that it is quite slow when working with very thick materials, although that is expected.; and that it also produces a lot of noise because of the fast mode.

This is what comes in the new Cricut Maker box:

- Cricut Maker machine.
- Fine-Point pen.
- Premium Fine-Point pen and housing.
- Rotary blade and drive housing.
- USB cable.
- Power adapter.
- LightGrip Mat 12" x 12".
- FabricGrip Mat 12" x 12".

- 50 ready-to-cut projects, which includes 25 sewing patterns.
- Materials for the first project.
- Welcome guide.

Which Cricut Model Should You Use?

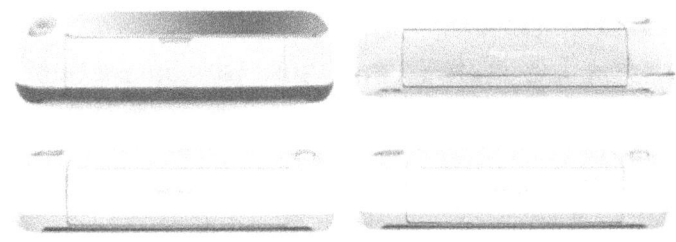

Photo credit: heyletsmakestuff.com

Although all Cricut models are great, the Cricut Maker or Explore Air models are highly recommended, whether you're a beginner or an advanced user. These two machines are usually ideal for most people, no matter the type of craft you use.

For the person who is looking to go into serious crafting, woodworking, sewing, and quilting, then the Cricut Maker is highly recommended. It is highly professional, and it can work for any craft that you're getting into. The system has a lot of benefits, especially on Design Space.

If you're a beginner who is looking to go deep into crafting, then you should also get the Cricut Maker because it will make no sense to purchase an old model, and then buy a new one when you have gained some experience.

You might be planning on using your Cricut machine for business purposes. This will mean that you will be repeating the same action occasionally. For this use, you can use the Cricut Explore Air 2 because it has a fast mode and many other advantages.

Beginners, leisurely crafters, and those who have a tight budget will work better with the Cricut Explore One and Explore Air.

Chapter 2. Cricut Tools And Accessories

Cricut Accessories

Cricut cutting machines come with quite a few accessories that you can purchase to add to the functionality of your machine. There are some accessories that most of the machines can use, and others that are designed only for a specific machine.

The following list of accessories will explain what the items are used for, and what machines they can be used on.

Cricut BrightPad

The Cricut BrightPad is a very handy device for serious crafters, as it illuminates projects to help with weeding, tracing, quilt blocks, paper piecing, and more. It can even help with jewelry making or model building.

The price is approx. $100.

The BrightPad is compatible with all of the Cricut machines and crafting materials.

- Cricut BrightPad Is Compatible With:

- All makes and models of Cricut Cutters.

- Cricut Bright Pad Is Not Compatible With:

- There are no Cricut machines whose device cannot be used alongside.

Cricut Cartridges

Cricut Cartridges are small cartridges that fit into the slots of some of the older Cricut machines (the Explore Air 2 still has a slot for them.) These cartridges were filled with images for purchase in order to expand a crafting image library.

You no longer need cartridges with current machines, and that is why Cricut has discontinued them. You can purchase digital cartridges from the Cricut craft shop website.

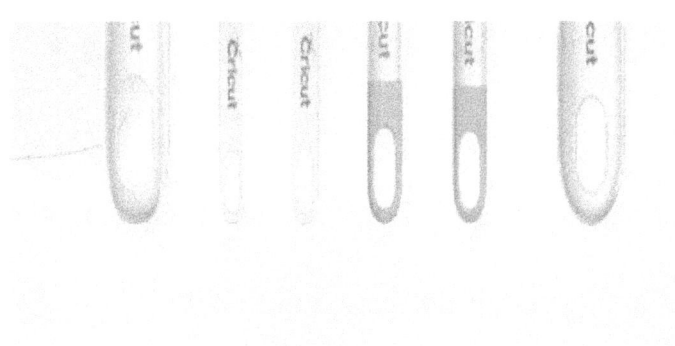

Like the physical cartridges, digital cartridges are sold in batches, which means you have to buy what comes with the pack. However, Design Space has thousands of images, projects, and more, that you can buy as individual items when you are creating your projects.

For those who already have cartridges, they are still able to be used. Design Space still supports them by letting you link cartridges once they have been loaded into the machine.

Although the Cricut Maker does not have a slot for cartridges, you can buy the Cricut USB cartridge adaptor for use with your purchased cartridges.

The Cricut Joy does not use cartridges and you cannot use the Cricut USB cartridge adapter with it.

- Cricut Cartridges Are Compatible With:
    - Cricut Explore.

- o Cricut Explore Air.

- o Cricut Explore Air 2.

- o Most older and legacy Cricut cutting machine models.

- Cricut Cartridges Are Not Compatible With:

    - o Cricut Joy.
    - o Cricut Maker (it needs an adaptor.)
    - o Cricut Cuttlebug.

Cricut Craft Tools

The Cricut Craft Tools have been specifically designed to make crafter's tasks a lot easier. As they are designed around the Cricut cutting machines, they make tasks like extra cutting, weeding, tweezing, tracing, etc., a breeze.

Each one of these tools, cutters, rulers, pens, knife blades, and so on can be purchased individually, or in various toolsets/bundles.

Most Cricut Tools come in standard colors such as cream or grey. There are exceptions and special promotions that may change the colors of the tools.

- Cricut Tools Are Compatible With:

    All makes and models of Cricut Cutters.

- Cricut Tools Are Not Compatible With:

There are no Cricut machines that the tools cannot be used alongside. The only tool that is not compatible with every cutting machine is the Cricut Stylus pen.

- Cricut Tool Colors:

Cricut Tools come in different colors that include:

- Blue.
- Mint.
- Gray.
- Lilac.
- Rose.
- Pink.
- Peach.

It should be noted that not all of the tools come in these colors, and the coloring can differ depending on the tool type.

Cricut Brayer

The brayer tool looks a bit like a lint roller. Although it does not remove lint, fluff, etc., it does help with sticking material firmly and smoothly to cutting mats.

The brayer helps the user to smooth the material, and press it firmly down onto cutting mats. It easily gets rid of wrinkles, kinks, bubbles, and can link blocks.

The price is approx. $20.

Cricut Distresser

This tool looks like the Cricut Scraper tool, except that it has two slits on either side of it. The distresser is used to give the paper a textured edge.

Cricut Fabric Shears

Cricut Fabric Shears cut through most fabric with ease, and this includes layered fabrics. The Fabric Shears are extra sharp with precision blades made from stainless steel.

They come with both right and left-handed comfort grip handles.

Cricut Leather Thimble

Cricut has cute leather thimbles to protect fingers when sewing.

Cricut Pin Cushion and Pins

Cricut Pin Cushion is soft and durable with a set of matching pins to help with sewing crafts.

Cricut Precision Piercer

This tool usually comes standard as part of the paper crafting toolset. You will need it if you are working with paper crafting for making flowers, swans, etc. The Precision Piercer allows crafters to put cuts, tiny holes, and other embellishments in the paper.

Cricut Quilting Tool

The Quilting Tool is one that most scrapbookers find incredibly useful. This tool creates professional look spirals and twirls that add extra polish to a project.

Cricut Measuring Tape

The Cricut Measuring Tape measures up to 60". It is a standard fabric measuring tape with the same measurements that you will find on the Design Space screen. This makes it easier to get the designs right for professional-looking craft finishes.

Cricut Rotary Cutter

The Cricut Rotary Cutter comes in two different sizes which are 45 mm and 60 mm. They have a carbon alloy steel rotary blade that slices through fabric like a knife through butter.

This is an excellent tool for precision slices of vinyl, leather, and most fabrics. The blade is replaceable. As the head can slide from left to right, it suits both left-handed and right-handed crafters.

Cricut Rulers

To make crafting more precise and professional, Cricut has a few different sized cutting rulers to make crafter's lives easier.

The cutting rulers sizes include:

- 18" x 24" ruler with a stainless steel straight cutting edge, non-slip base, and a protective grip.
- 12" x 24" clear acrylic design ruler.
- 6" x 26" clear acrylic design ruler.
- 3" x 18" clear acrylic design ruler.

Cricut Scissors

The Cricut Scissors are sharp 5" scissors that are ideal for any material, and they come with a protective case to protect the blades. They easily cut through vinyl, faux leather, paper, cardstock, and more.

They come with a left-handed or right-handed comfort grip handle.

Cricut Scoring Stylus Pen

The Scoring Stylus Pen is used for making fold lines in gift boxes, envelopes, and gift cards.

The Cricut Scoring Stylus Pen can be used by hand to create folds. It can also be used in the following Cricut cutting machines to create folds with a cut:

- Cricut Explore.

- Cricut Explore Air.

- Cricut Explore Air 2.

- Cricut Maker.

Cricut Scraper

The Cricut Scraper comes in a few different sizes: small, medium, and large. It is designed to help prolong the life of the Cricut cutting mats as it scrapes unwanted material off the surface.

This is also a good tool to use if you do not have a Brayer Tool, as it is a good burnishing tool. If you need to make sure that vinyl sticks down securely, run the scraper over it before pulling off of the transfer sheet.

Cricut Seam Ripper

This little tool allows for easy and effective removal of tiny stitches and seams without causing damage to the fabric.

Cricut Spatula

This little tool is a savior when you want to pick up an intricate cut. The tool allows a person to gently get under the image and lift it without tearing it. It is also a handy tool for getting off pieces that have become stuck on the mat, or backing sheet.

Cricut Thread Snips

The Cricut Thread Snips are sharp little snipping tools that quickly snip thread, or end pieces to neaten them up.

Cricut Trimmer

The Cricut Trimmer is a portable 12" trimmer with a precision blade and a 15" swing-out arm. The swing-out arm makes it easy to measure any type of material while the blade cuts effortlessly with precision through the materials.

There are blade replacements available in case the trimmer becomes blunt.

Cricut True Control Knife

The True Control Knife works pretty much the same as a carpenter's knife does. It has a lock-in adjustable blade for more material cutting control, and interchangeable blade sizes.

This knife can cut through a host of different materials including:

- Vinyl.
- Cardstock.
- Canvas.
- Fabrics.
- Leather.
- Paper.

Cricut Tweezer

There are a few kinds of tweezers offered by Cricut and these include:

- Cricut Broad tip Tweezers: The Cricut Broad tip Tweezers are ideal for material crafting, and to lift stubborn material from the cutting board. They are also useful for lifting up delicate cuts that the spatula may not be able to lift.

- Cricut Fine tip Tweezers: These Tweezers have a very fine edge that is needed for small intricate cuts that need to be cleaned up, or stuck down.

- Cricut Hook Tweezers: The Hook Tweezers can get into those awkward bends and twirls of some craft cuts. They are also good for removing larger craft pieces.

Cricut Weeder

The weeder looks like a little hook and is ideal for weeding out (neating) cut image designs. There are two different styles of weeders: the classic weeder and hook weeder. Although the classic weeder is a great starter weeder, and one that all crafters really need, more serious crafters will find the hook weeder really useful for those intricate designs.

Cricut Basic Tool Kit

The Cricut Basic Tool Kit includes the following tools:

- Cricut Scissors.

- Cricut Fine tip Tweezers.
- Cricut Classic Weeding Tool.
- Cricut Scraper (small.)
- Cricut Spatula.

Cricut Fabric/Sewing Tool Kit

The Cricut Fabric/Sewing Tool Kit includes the following tools:

- Cricut Fabric Shears.
- Cricut Seam Ripper.
- Cricut Leather Thimble.
- Cricut Measuring Tape.
- Cricut Snipper.
- Cricut Pincushion.
- Cricut Pins.
- Cricut Brayer Tool.
- Cricut Broad tip Tweezers.

Cricut Starter Tool Kit

The Cricut Starter Tool Kit includes the following tools:

- Cricut Classic Weeding Tool.
- Cricut Scraper (small.)
- Cricut Spatula.

Cricut Precision Cutting Kit

The Cricut Precision Cutting Tool Kit includes the following tools:

- Cricut True Control Knife.
- Cricut True Control Blades. (x 5)
- Cricut Blade Storage Cartridge.
- Cricut 18" x 24" Ruler.
- Cricut 12" x 12" self-healing crafting mat.

Cricut Paper Tool Kit

The Cricut Paper Tool Kit includes the following tools:

- Cricut Piercer.
- Cricut Quilting Tool.
- Cricut Edge Distresser.

Cricut 5" x 6" self-healing crafting mat

Cricut Essential Tool Kit

The Cricut Essential Tool Kit includes the following tools:

- Cricut Fine-Point Tweezer.
- Cricut Classic Weeding Tool.
- Cricut Spatula.
- Cricut Portable Trimmer.
- Cricut Scraper (small.)
- Cricut 5" Scissors for crafting.
- Cricut Stylus Scoring Pen.

Cricut Weeding/Vinyl Tool Kit

The Cricut Weeding/Vinyl Tool Kit includes the following tools:

- Cricut Piercer.
- Cricut Quilting Tool.
- Cricut Edge Distresser.
- Cricut 5" x 6" self-healing crafting mat.

Cricut Scraper and Spatula Kit

The Cricut Paper Tool Kit includes the following tools:

- Cricut Scraper (small.)
- Cricut Spatula.

Cricut Brayer and Remover Tool Kit

The Cricut Brayer and Remover Tool Kit include the following tools:

- Cricut Brayer Tool.
- Cricut Broad tip Tweezers.

Cricut Rotary Cutting Kit

The Cricut Rotary Cutting Tool Kit includes the following tools:

- Cricut Rotary Cutter (45mm.)
- Cricut 12" x 24" Acrylic Ruler (oversized.)
- Cricut 18" x 24" self-healing double-sided crafting mat.

Cricut True Control Knife Kit

The Cricut True Control Knife Tool Kit includes the following tools:

- Cricut True Control Knife.
- Cricut True Control Blades. (x 5)
- Cricut Blade Storage Cartridge.

Cricut Pens

There are two types of Cricut craft pens: the Freehand Pens and the Infusible Ink Pens. They come in different colors and sizes. Not all pens work with all Cricut machines.

Cricut Explore One Pen

The Cricut Explore One Pens come with the Pen Accessory Adapter that can be used with the Stylus Scoring Pen.

- Cricut Explore One Pens Are Compatible With:
    - Cricut Explore One.

- Cricut Explore One Pens Are Not Compatible With:
    - Any other Cricut machines.

Cricut Ultimate Gel Pens

The Cricut Ultimate Gel Pens come in different colors and pen sizes.

- Cricut Ultimate Gel Pens Are Compatible With:
    - Cricut Maker.
    - Cricut Explore Air family.
    - Cricut Explore One (these pens require an adapter for the Explore One.)

- Cricut Ultimate Gel Pens Are Not Compatible With:
    - Older Cricut machines.
    - Cricut Joy.

Cricut Extra Fine-Point Pens

The Cricut Extra Fine-Point pens come in different colors and pen sizes.

- Cricut Extra Fine-Point Pens Are Compatible With:
    - Cricut Maker.

- Cricut Explore Air family.

- Cricut Explore One (these pens require an adapter for the Explore One.)

- Cricut Extra Fine-Point Pens Are Not Compatible With:

    - Older Cricut machines.

    - Cricut Joy.

Cricut Milky Gel Pens

The Cricut Milky Gel Pens come in different colors and pen sizes.

- Cricut Milky Gel Pens Are Compatible With:

    - Cricut Maker.

    - Cricut Explore Air family.

    - Cricut Explore One (these pens require an adapter for the Explore One.)

- Cricut Milky Gel Pens Are Not Compatible With:

    - Older Cricut machines.

    - Cricut Joy.

Cricut Glitter Gel Pens

The Cricut Glitter Gel Pens come in different colors and pen sizes.

- Cricut Glitter Gel Pens Are Compatible With:

    o Cricut Maker.

    o Cricut Explore Air family.

    o Cricut Explore One (these pens require an adapter for the Explore One.)

- Cricut Glitter Gel Pens Are Not Compatible With:

    o Older Cricut machines.

    o Cricut Joy.

Cricut Infusible Ink Freehand Markers Pens

The Cricut Infusible Ink Freehand Marker Pens come in watercolors and normal marker pens. They come in different colors and pen sizes.

- Cricut Infusible Ink Freehand Markers Pens Are Compatible With:

    o EasyPress.

    o EasyPress 2.

    o EasyPress Mini.

- Cricut Infusible Ink Freehand Marker Pens Are Not Compatible With:

  o These pens cannot be used with any Cricut cutting machine.

Cricut Joy Pens

The following pens are not compatible with any of the other Cricut cutting machines. These pens are only for use with the Cricut Joy:

- Cricut Joy Infusible Ink Pens in different colors and point sizes.

- Cricut Joy Gel Pens in different colors and point sizes.
- Cricut Joy Glitter Gel Pens in different colors and sizes.
- Cricut Joy Metallic Markers in different colors and sizes.
- Cricut Joy Extra Fine-Point Pens in different colors.

Cricut Craft Mats

Cricut has self-healing craft mats designed specifically for crafting. It must be noted that these mats are NOT for use as cutting mats. They are purely for cutting and working with material out of the cutting machines.

They are called self-healing mats because they close up when you cut through them. The Cricut mats have twice the self-healing power than most self-healing craft mats on the market.

These mats come double-sided with useful gridlines, numbers, and angles for 30°, 60°, and 90° angle markings on them. These craft mats come in an array of colors. Depending on the type and style of the mat, colors may include:

- Rose.
- Lilac.
- Blue.
- Mint.
- Gray.
- Patterned.
- Black.

The self-healing mats come in sizes that include:

- 12" x 12".
- 18" x 24".
- 24" x 36".

As they are not to be used in a Cricut cutting machine, you can buy these mats for use with your crafts, no matter which cutting machine you have.

Cricut Cutting Mats

All of the latest Cricut cutting machines, except for the Cricut Joy, use cutting mats to cut material. There are four standard mats that are used in these machines. The Cricut Joy does not need mats for some cuts, but there are cuts where that do require a cutting mat. The Cricut Joy needs special mats due to its size and is not compatible with the standard mats used by other Cricut cutting machines.

Standard Cricut Cutting Mats

There are four standard Cricut Cutting Mats; each mat has a different purpose and comes in one or more sizes. These mats are as follows:

- LightGrip mat—Blue.
    - Sizes: 12" x 12", 12" x 24", and 6" x 12".
    - Material Weight: Lightweight materials.
    - Materials: Washi tape sheets, wrapping paper, thin cardstock, printer paper, vellum, and scrapbook paper (thin sheets.)

- Standard Grip mat—Green.
  - Sizes: 12" x 12", 12" x 24", and 6" x 12".
  - Material Weight: Medium weight materials.
  - Materials: Cardstock textured paper, embossed cardstock, vinyl, and iron-on vinyl.
- StrongGrip mat—Purple.
  - Sizes: 12" x 12", 12" x 24", and 6" x 12".
  - Material Weight: Heavyweight materials.
  - Materials: Poster boards, faux leather, faux suede, corrugated cardboard, chipboard, metal, stiff fabrics, leather, thick cardstock, glitter cardstock, and mosaic vinyl.
- FabricGrip mat—Pink.
  - Sizes: Sizes: 12" x 12", 12" x 24", and 6" x 12".
  - Material Weight: Fabrics, as well as layered fabrics.
  - Materials: Fabric.

Cricut Joy Cutting Mats

The Cricut Joy has its own specific cutting mats that do not work with any other Cricut cutting machines. It should be noted that none of the standard cutting mats work with the Cricut Joy.

The Cricut Joy Cutting Mats include the following mats:

- Cricut Joy Card Mat—Blue.

  - Sizes: 4.5" x 6.25".

  - Materials: Cardstock, paper, and materials to make greeting cards.

- Cricut Joy Standard Grip Mat—Green.

  - Sizes: 4.5" x 12" and 4.5" x 6.5".

  - Material Weight: Medium weight materials.

  - Materials: Cardstock textured paper, embossed cardstock, vinyl, and iron-on vinyl.

- Cricut Joy LightGrip Mat—Blue.

  - Sizes: 4.5" x 12" and 4.5" x 6.5".

  - Material Weight: Lightweight materials.

- Materials: Cardstock, paper, and other lightweight materials.

Cricut EasyPress Mats

For heat transfers, the EasyPress Mats are the better option to choose over an ironing board. Even if you do not have the EasyPress or one of the new EasyPresses, if you are crafting and using iron-on or heat transfers, you should invest in one of these mats. Their flat, durable surface is what makes getting the transfer on correctly a lot easier than a conventional ironing board.

The Cricut EasyPress mats come in four sizes and are compatible with all EasyPress irons and mini irons.

EasyPress Mat Sizes:

- Extra-large sized mat: 20" x 16".
- Large-sized mat: 14" x 14".
- Medium-sized mat: 12" x 12".
- Small-sized mat: 8" x 10".

Cricut Machine Tools

The Cricut machine comes with blades and blade housings that are used for different cutting purposes as well as materials. While the larger Cricut cutting machines have a few blades and blade housings that are universal to them, there are a few blades that are specific to that machine.

Cricut Cutting Machine Blade

The cutting machine's cutting blade has two to four parts to it and these are:

- Blade: The blade looks similar to a nail or thick pin. There are a few types of blades that are used for the cutting of different materials. Blades can be replaced as they can become blunt through a lot of continuous use. The blade has a plastic protective tip at the top that extends into the blade at the bottom.

- Blade Housing: The blade is inserted into the housing. The housing fits into the accessory clamp inside of the cutting machine. The clamp holds and guides the blade.

- Drive Housing: The Cricut Maker has more specialized blades that use the Cricut Adaptive Tool System. The drive housing is what helps to drive the gear that sits on top of the various Cricut Maker blade housings. The blade housings, for some of the Cricut Maker blades, look a lot different than more standard blades. They can be identified by a gold wheel on top of the silver blade housing.

- Blade Tips: The QuickSwap drive housing comes with interchangeable blade tips instead of nail type blades.

Bonded-Fabric Blade

This blades' color is pink, and should not be used on any other materials except bonded fabrics.

- The blade works with the following Cricut cutting machines:
    - Cricut Maker.
    - Cricut Explore family.
    - Cricut Explore Air family (Air and Air 2.)

- The material that can be cut with this blade includes the following:
    - Burlap.
    - Cotton.
    - Denim.
    - Felt.
    - Oil Cloth.
    - Polyester.
    - Silk.
    - Faux Leather.

- Housing for the blade:

    - Pink Bonded-Fabric blade housing.

    - Silver or gold Fine-Point blade housing.

- Cutting mat(s):

    - FabricGrip mat (pink.)

    - Standard Grip mat (green.)

Deep-Point Blade

This blade's color is black and it can be used for cutting materials that need deeper cuts.

- The blade works with the following Cricut cutting machines:

    - Cricut Maker.
    - Cricut Explore family.

    - Cricut Explore Air family (Air and Air 2.)

- The material that can be cut with this blade includes the following:

    - Aluminum Foil.

    - Craft Foam.

- Corrugated Cardboard/Paper.
- Leather.
- Metallic Leather.
- Magnetic Sheet (up to 0.6mm).

- Housing for the blade:
  - Black Deep-Point blade housing.

- Cutting mat(s):
  - Standard Grip mat (green.)
  - StrongGrip mat (purple.)

Fine-Point Blade

This blade's color is white. It is the standard blade and housing that comes with all Cricut cutting machines. The Fine-Point blades with the white caps are for the newer machines, while the ones with the gray caps are for older Cricut cutting machines.

- The blade works with the following Cricut cutting machines:
  - Cricut Maker.
  - Cricut Explore family.
  - Cricut Explore Air family (Air and Air 2.)

- The material that can be cut with this blade includes the following:

- Canvas.
- Cardstock.
- Fine Faux Leather.
- Glitter Vinyl.
- Holographic Vinyl.
- Heat Transfer Vinyl. (HTV)
- Iron-on Vinyl.
- Light Chipboard
- Outdoor Vinyl.
- Parchment Paper.
- Printable Vinyl.
- Tattoo Paper.
- Vellum.
- Washi Tape.
- Window Stick.

- Housing for the blade:
  - The pink Bonded-Fabric blade housing.

- Rose, silver, or gold Fine-Point blade housing.

- Cutting mat(s):

  - LightGrip mat (blue.)
  - Standard Grip mat (green.)
  - StrongGrip mat (purple.)

Knife Blade

This knife blade is silver and comes with the wheel gear housing.

- The blade works with the following Cricut cutting machines:

  - Cricut Maker.

- The material that can be cut with this blade includes the following:

  - Balsa wood that is either 1/16" or 3/32".
  - Basswood that is either 1/16" or 1/32".
  - Heavy chipboard up to 2.0mm.
  - Matboard 4 ply.

- Housing for the blade:

  - Silver gear wheel housing.

- Cutting mat(s):

  - Standard Grip mat (green.)

- o StrongGrip mat (purple.)

QuickSwap Debossing Tip

This blade tip uses the QuickSwap housing which is silver. Debossing is the process of creating indented imprints in materials. This tip makes beautiful intricate designs effortlessly.

- The blade works with the following Cricut cutting machines:

  - o Cricut Maker.

- The material that can be cut with this blade includes the following:

  - o Balsa Wood that is either 1/16" or 3/32".

  - o Chipboard (heavy) up to 2 mm.

  - o Chipboard (light) up to 0.37 mm.

  - o Cardstock (heavy and light).

  - o Faux Leather (very thin).

  - o Foil Acetate.

  - o Glitter Cardstock Craft Foam.

  - o Kraft Board.

  - o Leather.

- Matboard (4 plies.)
- Poster Board Foil, normal, and metallic.
- Tooling Leather.
- Vellum.

- Housing for the blade:
  - QuickSwap housing with gold gear.

- Cutting mat(s):
  - Standard Grip mat (green.)
  - StrongGrip mat (purple.)

QuickSwap Engraving Tip

This blade tip uses the QuickSwap housing that is silver. The engraving tip takes the Cricut Maker to a different level, as with this you can actually engrave certain materials with the cutting machine.

- The blade works with the following Cricut cutting machines:
  - Cricut Maker

- The material that can be cut with this blade includes the following:
  - Acetate.
  - Anodized Aluminum.
  - Brass.
  - Bronze.
  - Faux Leather.
  - Foil Acetate.
  - Leather.
  - Stainless Steel.
  - Tooling Leather.
  - Vellum.
- Housing for the blade:
  - QuickSwap housing with gold gear.
- Cutting mat(s):
  - Standard Grip mat (green.)
  - StrongGrip mat (purple.)

QuickSwap Perforation Blade

This blade tip uses the QuickSwap housing which is silver. The Cricut Maker gives crafters a professional edge with unique blades like the perforation blade. This blade allows the crafter to create perforated materials for items like tear-off raffle tickets, journal pages, booklets with tear-out pages, and so on.

- The blade works with the following Cricut cutting machines:
    - Cricut Maker.

- The material that can be cut with this blade includes the following:
    - Acetate and Foil Acetate.
    - Craft Foam; normal and glitter craft foam.
    - Cardstock; heavy and corrugated.
    - Faux Leather (very thin).
    - Felt.
    - Iron-on materials.
    - Poster board normal and metallic.
    - Plastic.
    - Tooling Leather.
    - Vellum.

- Housing for the blade:
    - QuickSwap housing with gold gear.

- Cutting mat(s):

    o Standard Grip mat (green.)

    o StrongGrip mat (purple.)

Quick Swap Wavy Blade

This blade tip uses the QuickSwap housing which is silver. This handy wheel makes wavy lines on the material and it can cut your material in wavy lines as well.

- The blade works with the following Cricut cutting machines:

    o Cricut Maker.

- The material that can be cut with this blade includes the following:

    o Cardstock; heavy and glitter.
    o Cotton Denim.
    o Corrugated Cardboard.
    o Flannel.
    o Fleece.
    o Kraft Board.
    o Poster Board.

- Housing for the blade:

    o QuickSwap housing with gold gear.

- Cutting mat(s):

    o Standard Grip mat (green.)

    o StrongGrip mat (purple.)

Scoring Wheel

The scoring wheel is much like the Stylus Scoring Pen, except it makes an edgier line, and comes in two different point sizes: 01 and 02. The tip chosen will depend on the material you are using.

- The blade works with the following Cricut cutting machines:

    o Cricut Maker

- The material that can be cut with this blade includes the following:

    o Tip 01: Lighter materials like those used with the blue LightGrip mat or green Standard Grip mat.

        - Cardstock.

        - Paper.

        - Vinyl.

- Tip 02: This tip is better suited to heavier or coated materials that require the StrongGrip mat (purple) or Bonded-Fabric mat (pink.)

    - Glitter Cardstock.
    - Bonded Materials.
    - Poster board like the metallic version.
    - Chipboard (light.)

- Housing for the blade:
    - Silver gear wheel housing.

- Cutting mat(s):
    - LightGrip mat (blue.)
    - Standard Grip mat (green.)
    - StrongGrip mat (purple.)

Cricut Joy Fine-Point Blade

The Cricut Joy uses a Fine-Point blade that is not interchangeable and can only be used with the Joy.

- The blade works with the following Cricut cutting machines:
    - Cricut Joy

- The material that can be cut with this blade includes the following:
  - Cardstock.
  - Cardstock Glitter.
  - Copy Paper.
  - Corrugated Cardboard.
  - Insert Cards.
  - Smart Iron-on Materials.
  - Smart Materials.
  - Poster Board (foil.)
  - Vinyl and Writable Vinyl.
- Housing for the blade:
  - Sliver housing with a white cap.
- Cutting mat(s):
  - FabricGrip mat (pink.)
  - Standard Grip mat (green.)

Cricut Storage Bags

In order to keep your machine safe and in good shape, there are a lot of good storage bag options for the machines. Some of these bags also make it easy to transport the Cricut machine without causing damage.

If you need to use your machine on the go, there are some good options to take your materials, tools, and accessories too.

Cutting Machine Totes

Cricut offers some beautiful tote bags to store the Cricut machines in. These totes come in various colors, and there are a few different sizes.

There is a standard size for larger machines such as the Explore family including the Explore Air and Explore Air 2. These totes are also compatible with the Cricut Maker, and some of the older model cutting machines.

The Cricut Joy has its own protective tote in grey and teal to match the machine.

EasyPress Totes

The EasyPress tote makes it easy to store and protect the Cricut EasyPress. There are two different-sized totes: the 9" x 9" for the smaller EasyPress machines, and the 12" x 10" for the larger EasyPress machines.

Rolling Craft Tote

The Cricut Rolling Craft Tote is not designed for the actual machine, but it is a really handy solution to store all of your crafting materials and tools in. Plus, it has wheels which make it easy to move around, and make it portable. The Rolling Craft Totes come in various colors and provide a wonderful space to neatly organize your crafting materials.

Chapter 3. Materials That Can Be Used For Cricut

The Cricut materials range has grown over the years, and with the introduction of the Cricut Maker, it can now cut even more materials such as metal, leather, and even wood.

Infusible Ink

This is a relatively new type of material for the Cricut range, and it has become really popular with crafters, but it is only available for use with the Cricut Maker and Cricut Joy at the moment. It gives smooth prints onto a fabric that make it look like they have been professionally dyed.

The Infusible Ink range does not only stop at the magnificent inks but comes with a lot of blanks that can be used with the ink. These include:

- T-Shirts.

- Baby Onesies.

- Canvas Tote Bags.

- Coaster Rounds.

- Coaster Squares.

The infusible ink itself comes in the following forms:

- Pens.

- Transfer Sheets.

- Cricut Joy Transfer Sheets.

Iron-On

Iron-On is one of the most popular Cricut materials as it can be used on cushions, clothes, bedding, towels, and so on. Cricut has hundreds of different colors and types, which include:

- Everyday Iron-On.
- Heat Transfer Vinyl.
- Glitter Iron-On.
- Foil Iron-On.
  - Printable Iron-On.

Leather

There are a few different types of leather that some of the cutting machines can cut, and this includes the following leather types:

- Faux Suede.
- Genuine Leather.
- Pebbled Faux Leather.
- Soft Metallic Leather.
- Tooling Leather.

Metal

The new engraving tool and the Knife Blade make it possible to cut metal, which includes:

- Aluminum Sheets.
- Bronze.
- Copper.
- Gold.
- Silver.

Others

There are a lot of different materials that can be cut with the Cricut cutting machines besides the obvious ones. These materials include:

- Party Foil.
- Chipboard.
- Balsa Wood.
- Wood Veneer.

- Window Cling.
- Felt.
- Foam.
- Fabric.
- Bonded Fabric.

Paper

There are more than 11 types of paper, each with at least 5, or move different variations of each type. Cricut cutting machines paper materials include:

- Adhesive-Backed Deluxe Paper.
- Insert Cards.
- Cardstock.
- Glitter Cardstock.
- Corrugated Cardboard.
- Foil Embossed.
- Kraft Board.
- Scrapbook.
- Pearl.
- Poster Board.
- Sparkle or Shimmer Paper.

Vinyl

There are many types of vinyl that can be cut with the Cricut cutting machines, and these include:

- Cricut Joy Smart Vinyl.
- Everyday Vinyl.
- Glitter Vinyl.
- Mosaic Vinyl.
- Holographic Vinyl.
- Party Foil.
- Premium Vinyl Range.
- Premium Outdoor Vinyl.
- Sticker Material.
- Tattoo Material.
- Stencil Vinyl.
- Linen Vinyl.
- Removable Vinyl.
- Permanent Vinyl.
- Metallic Vinyl.
- Textured Vinyl.
- Textured Metallic Vinyl.

Chapter 4. Design Space Application

Design Space On Mobile Device

The Cricut Design Space is cloud-based, and you can pick up your project across various platforms. Here's how you can download the latest version (v 3.18.1) of this application on your mobile devices:

- Apple App Store (iOS): Simply search for "Cricut" on the App Store from your iPhone or iPad, and select "GET" to begin the download. You can then easily login with your registered Cricut ID to continue working on your projects on your phone.

- Google Play (Android): You can search for "Cricut" on Google Play from your Android Phone or Tablet. Then select "Install" to begin the download. Once completed, use your Cricut ID to login, and pick up your projects and ideas where you left off.

How to Install/Uninstall Design Space?

Let us tackle how to install/uninstall on these platforms including Windows, Mac, iOS, and Android devices.

Install on Windows/Mac

- Click on your browser and navigate to www.design.cricut.com.
- If you are a first time user, you need to create a Cricut ID, otherwise, sign in with your Cricut ID. Ensure that the page is fully loaded before carrying out this activity in order to avoid an error.
- Select "New Project."
- Select "Download Plugin" from the prompt.
- Wait for the download to finish, and then select the downloaded file to Open/Run it.
- Click "Next" when the Cricut installer opens.
- Read the "Terms of Use," and accept the agreement.
- Click "Install" to begin the installation.
- Click "Done" at the end of the installation.

Install the Cricut Design Space App on iOS

- Tap on the App Store icon on your device.
- Search for Cricut Design Space.
- Tap the "Get" button to download. Please confirm the download with your iTunes password if prompted. The app

will launch and display the necessary options that will be used to complete the process.

Install the Cricut Design Space App on Android

- Tap Google Play Store App on your device to open it.
- Search for Cricut Design Space.
- Tap on the "Install" button.
- Tap on the Cricut Design Space icon to open it when the installation is complete.
- Sign in, and start designing your project.

Uninstall Cricut Design Space on iOS

- Press and hold the Design Space icon on your iOS device till it vibrates
- Press the "X" button to delete it from your device. This is very easy, right?

Uninstall Cricut Design Space App on Android

- Go to "Settings."
- Tap on "Apps" or "Applications."
- Swipe to the "Download" tab or "Application Manager."
- Search for the App you intend to uninstall.
- Tap the "Uninstall" button to finish and the App is gone for good.

Uninstall on Mac

- Move to Finder and open the "Applications" folder.
- Search for Cricut Design Space.
- Drag it to "Trash."
- Right-click on the "Trashcan" and select "Empty Trash" to remove the Application.

Uninstall on Windows

- Click on the "Start" button.
- Select "Settings."
- Select "Application."
- Look for Cricut Design Space and choose "Uninstall."

How to Center Your Designs to Cut in Cricut Design Space?

- Sign in to the Cricut Design section. Click on the "New Project."
- Click "Download."
- Click "Upload Picture."
- Click "Browse."
- Save your picture.
- Select the saved image, and insert an image.
- Select the picture. Click on it.

- As you can see, the picture is automatically moved to the upper left corner.
- To prevent this, you can fool the software by placing the image in the center of your design area and the mat. This is useful if you want to create openings in the middle of a page.
- Click on the shape tool.
- Create a shape of 11.5 x 11.5 inches.
- Select the square and change the setting to cut it in the drawing.
- The square now appears as an outline.
- Click "Align" and "Center" with the selected pattern and square.
- Click the arrow of the size of your square and resize it without moving the top left corner to reduce the size of the square.
- Select the square and pattern, then click "Attach." Click on it.
- As you can see now, the design is centered.

How to Write with Sketch Pens in Cricut Design Space?

- Sign in to the Cricut Design section. Create a new project.
- Click "Download."
- Select upload a picture.
- Click "Browse."

- Open your file, then save. To get a good effect, use a file with thin lines and no large spaces.
- Click on the pattern, and paste it.
- Select the pattern.
- Change the drawing to a drawing.
- You will now see the drawing as an outline drawn.
- Click on it.
- Your drawing will now be displayed on the cutting screen. Click on "Continue."
- If you change your drawing to draw, the software automatically selects the pen tool. Insert the pen or marker into the recommended clip. Insert paper and click on the start icon.
- The pen now draws your pattern.

How to Upload PNG File?

After you've converted your PDF document to PNG file format, there are some ways to clean up the file before printing, and then crop it with Cricut Design Space.

- Click "Create New Project."
- Click "Upload Picture."
- Click on the image to upload.
- Click "Browse."
- The "Open File" dialog box opens. Select the PNG file you want to upload and click.

- An example of a picture can be found in Cricut Design Space. Since we want to edit this file, we select "Complex Image" and click "Next."
- The PNG file is loaded into Cricut Design Space. Select and Delete.

How to Convert a PDF to PNG Format?

- After downloading the PDF document to your computer, open your browser and go to png2pdf.com.
- Click on the upload files.
- The "Open File" dialog box starts. Locate the PDF file to convert (probably in the "Downloads" folder,) click the PDF file, and then the file is uploaded. You should see a progress bar. Once the file has been uploaded and converted, a "Download" button appears below the small image of the uploaded file.
- Click on "Download." The file is going to be downloaded as a ZIP file and should appear in the status bar at the bottom of the screen. Just click on the filename to open the ZIP file.
- The "Open File" dialog opens, and the downloaded file should be displayed. Since the file is still in ZIP format, you must first unzip, or unzip it. Just click "Extract All Files."
- The "Open File" dialog opens, and your newly converted PDF file should be displayed in a PNG file. You can open the file with a double-click if you only want to see what the file looks like. Close the window now by clicking on the red "X."

- After you have converted your PDF file to PNG format, you must upload the PNG file to Cricut Design Space so that you can use the "Print" and "Cut" functions.

Working with Edit Bar in Cricut Design Space

Here are important terminologies to help our understanding of the Design Space Edit Bar, that will have to be defined. A word of caution though is that some of the terms used here are common tools for everyday use on the computer so it shouldn't be difficult to understand but our level of computer literacy is not the same. Therefore, pardon me if you already know many of them. This has been done for the sake of those who do not know. The terms are as follows:

- Undo/Redo: Refers to undoing any change made to the layer, or redo any priorly taken undone action.

- Linetype: Refers to how the machine will interact with the material on the mat including cut, draw, and score as described below.

- Cut: Refers to a cutting layer with the aid of a blade from your material.

- Draw: Refers to drawing the layer with the aid of a Cricut pen.

- Score: Refers to scoring the layer using a Scoring Stylus or Scoring Wheel.

- Linetype Swatch: Refers to choosing additional attributes that your layer will use. There are different types of options you can select from based on the selected Linetype (cut, draw, and score.)

Working with Fonts in Design Space

The ability to personalize a project with the use of distinct fonts and text is one of the unique features of the Cricut Design Space. Why is this unique? Because it gives you the freedom to express the creativity of your mind. This creative ability is innate in us, and there is this satisfaction accompanied by a great sense of accomplishment that is felt whenever the projects are delivered to taste.

The Cricut Design Space has another amazing feature which is the ability to change the font after ungrouping or isolating the letters, you can use the Cricut fonts or the one installed on your computer or device.

How to Select Font?

If you have ever worked with the Image Edit Tool before, then you will definitely be at home with the Text Edit tool in Cricut Design

Space. This is because the two tools are similar in their mode of operation in rotating, sizing, and positioning of text. The similarity of the tools will excite you because it makes the job simpler when editing the text and locating the right font. With this, you can personalize projects easily.

How to Edit Fonts?

The Edit bar in Cricut Design Space grants you access to edit the features of particular images or text. These features include Linetype, Size, Rotate, Fill, Position, and Mirror. There are additional options in the Text layers including Line Spacing, Font Styles, and Letter Spacing. So how do you edit the font? Here, I will show you.

Select the text object you want to edit on the Canvas, or you can insert text from the design panel, or select a text layer from the Layers Panel. Once it is selected, the Text Edit Bar will pop up directly below "Standard Edit Bar." Note that the "Standard Edit Bar" will be hidden when you are not interacting with the text.

When the "Text Edit Bar" pops up, you can begin to manipulate the font using the options described below. Simple right?

How to Add Text to Cricut Design Space?

Navigate to the left-hand side of the Canvas and select the Text tool. When the Text tool is selected, the font list will open if you are using iOS/Android, or the Text bar and text box will pop up for users with Windows/Mac.

Select the desired font size and the font type you intend to use, and then input your text. If you intend to start on a new line of text on the same textbox, use the "Return" key after the prior line of text. Do not freak out when you did not choose the font setting before typing the text, with Cricut Design Space, it is possible to type the text before selecting the font on a Windows/Mac computer.

- Click or tap on any area outside the text box to close it.
- To edit the text is pretty simple. Double click on the text to display available options.
- The Edit bar is found at the top of the Canvas for Windows/Mac users, and at the bottom of the Canvas for iOS/Android users.

How to Troubleshoot Error Codes in the Cricut Design Space?

Every electronic device pops up error when there is a conflict with its program. The Cricut Design Space is no exception because it is also a program running on your device, and will also complain if something is missing from its chain of command. As a user interface, it will report this error to you for correction in order to complete its current task.

Let us describe some of these errors and how to troubleshoot them. If you still cannot solve the problem after going through these steps, or the error is not treated here, please feel free to contact Customer Care.

Error (0)

- Restart your computer and machine.
- If your device is short of that then, ensure that your computer or device satisfies these minimum requirements, or try to use another computer or device that meets the requirements.
- Clear your cache, browser history, cookies, and ensure that your browser is updated to the current version.
- Recreate the project if only one and not multiple projects is affected.
- Use another computer or device if the above troubleshooting options fail.

Error (-11): "Device Authentication" Error

- Close all background programs on your computer or device, and then try again.
- Check to see that your browser is updated to the current version.

Error (-18): "Device Timeout" Error

- Switch off your computer or device.
- Close Design Space.
- Restart the Design Space.
- Power on the Cricut Maker, and then try to cut again.
- If no solution, contact Member Care.

Error (-21): "Data Transmission" Error

- Clear your cache, browser history, and cookies.
- Close your browser, re-launch it again, and then try cutting.
- Use a different browser to try cut.
- Check your internet speed, and ensure that it meets the minimum requirement.
- Contact your Internet Service Provider (ISP) for assistance.

Error (-24): "Ping Timeout" Error

- Recreate the project because it is possible that the project file is too large, or is not properly saved.
- Try another USB port on the computer, or make use of Bluetooth.
- Use a different USB cable.
- Check your internet speed.
- If nothing works, try a different computer.

Error (-32): "Firmware Not Available" Error

- Since this error pops up only when there is a compatibility problem, check the connectivity of your device to the Cricut machine.
- If you are 100% sure that the connectivity is correct, then contact Member Care for assistance.

Error (-33): "Invalid Material Setting" Error

- Check the Smart Set Dial. This error appears when there is no selected material from the Design Space and the Smart Set Dial is set to "Custom." Therefore, ensure that the material is selected from the Design Space material drop-down menu.
- Try a different material setting.
- Contact Member Care for assistance.

Design Space Canvas

Purchasing a Cricut is futile if you don't learn exactly how to master Style Room, since you will always require this software to cut any kind of job. In my opinion, Cricut Style Room is an exceptional device for newbies, and also if you have no experience with any other Layout programs like Photoshop or Illustrator, you will certainly discover that although it looks overwhelming, it's quite simple.

Layout Space it's mainly to touch up your projects and create marginal designs with forms and fonts.

If you desire something a lot more innovative, you are most likely to need your own designs or Cricut Accessibility. That's a subscription where you obtain access to their supergiant library. Find out more about it in this write-up and also the guide I create.

When you log into your Cricut Design Area account and also intend to start or modify a new project, you will certainly do every little thing from a window called Canvas. The Canvas Location in Cricut Style Space is where you do all of your modifications prior to you cut your tasks. I get it!

There are numerous switches, options, and points to do that you might feel shed. Do not worry, I am below along the way, applauding you up and motivating you to maintain going. In this publication, you are about to learn what each and every single symbol on the Canvas area is for. To keep every little thing in order as well as easy to understand, we are going to divide the canvas into 4 areas, and also 4 colors:

- Top Panel Yellow: Modifying Area.
- Left Panel Blue: Insert Location.
- Right Panel Purple: Layers Panel.
- Green: Canvas Location.

Pointer: This is not a short message, so I encourage you to get a cup of coffee with some donuts or cookies if possible.

Top Panel Cricut Design Space

The top panel in the Style Space Canvas area is for editing, enhancing, and preparing aspects of the Canvas area. From this panel, you can pick what type of font style you'd like to use; you can transform dimensions, straighten styles, as well as extra! This panel is divided into 2 sub-panels. The very first one permits you to save, name, and finally reduce your jobs; and also the second one will enable you to regulate, and also modify points on the Canvas area.

Sub-Panel #1: Name Your Project and Cut it

This sub-panel enables you to navigate from the Canvas to your account, projects, as well as it additionally sends your completed projects to cut.

- **Toggle Menu:** When you click on this button, one more entire menu will move open. This menu is a useful one. However, it's not part of the Canvas, and that's why I won't be entering into a lot of detail. Primarily, from here you can most likely go to your profile, and also transform your photo.

There are various other useful and technological points you can do from this Menu like calibrating your maker blades; additionally, updating the Firmware (Software) of your tool. Furthermore, you can manage your memberships from Cricut Accessibility, your account details, and also more. I suggest you to click on every web link to make sure that you discover every little thing that Cricut Style Room has for you.

Note: On the settings chosen, you can transform the visibility as well as measurements of the Canvas; this is explained much better at the end of this article when I describe everything about the canvas area.

- **My Projects:** When you click "My Projects," you will certainly be rerouted to your collection of points you have currently developed; this is excellent because often you may wish to re-cut a previously developed job. So, there's no need for you to recreate the same job over and over.

- **Save:** This option will certainly turn on after you've placed one component on your canvas area. I suggest you save your project as you go. Although the software program is on the cloud, if your browser accidents, there goes your hard work with it.

- **Maker—Explore (Machine):** Depending upon the sort of Cricut you have you will certainly require to select either the Cricut Maker or the Cricut Explore Machine; this is really crucial because on the Cricut Manufacturer you will discover choices that are only readily available to that specific Cricut. So, if you have a Maker, and you are making with the Explore alternative ON, you won't be able to turn on the tools that are for the Maker.

- **Make It:** When you are done posting your files, and also ready to cut, click on "Make it." Your tasks are separated by mats according to the colors of your task. From this home window, you can likewise boost the variety of projects to cut; this is excellent if you are planning on developing greater than one cut.

Sub-Panel # 2: Modifying Font Selections

It's incredibly useful, and also it will certainly help you to modify, prepare, and also organize font styles as well as pictures on the Canvas Location.

- **Undo & Redo:** Occasionally while we work, we make blunders. These little buttons are a great means to correct them. Click "Undo" when you develop something you do not like, or make a mistake. Click "Redo" when you inadvertently remove something you didn't wish to erase or modify. (If only there were something comparable forever itself lol.)

- **Line Type and Fill:** This option will inform your equipment what tools as well as blades you are going to utilize. Bear in mind that relying on the Maker you have actually picked on the top of the home window (Manufacturer or Discover,) you will have different choices.
- **Line Type:** This alternative will inform your device when you are cutting your job, what device you will certainly be using. Right now, there are seven choices (Cut, Draw, Score, Engrave, Wave, Deboss, and Perf.) If you have a Cricut Maker, all options will certainly be readily available, although if you have an Explore, you will only have the Cut, Draw, and the Score choice. Right here is a much more comprehensive description of each tool:

    - **Cut:** Unless you published a JPEG or PNG photo to the Canvas; "Cut" is the default line type that every one of your elements on your canvas will certainly have; this means that when you press "Make It," your maker will certainly cut those designs.

    With the Cut choice chosen, you can transform the fill of your components, at the end of the day, this converts into the different shades of materials you will certainly utilize when you cut your jobs.

- **Draw:** If you intend to create on your layouts, you can do it with your Cricut. When you appoint this line type, you will certainly be prompted to choose any one of the Cricut Pens you have (You require detailed pens, unless you have a 3rd event adapter.) When you select a specific layout, the layers on your Canvas area will certainly be outlined with the shade of the pen you picked. With this tool, when you click "Make It," rather than reducing, your Cricut will certainly create or draw. Keep in mind: This option doesn't tint your styles.

- **Score:** Score is an extra powerful version of the "Rating Line" situated on the left panel. When you appoint this attribute to a layer, every one of the designs will certainly show up scored or rushed. This time, when you click "Make It." Your Cricut won't cut, yet it will score your products. However, keep in mind the wheel just collaborates with the Cricut Manufacturer.

- **Engrave, Deboss, Wave, as well as Perf:** These are the newest tools that Cricut has released for the Cricut Maker, and with them, you will have the ability to create incredible results on various sorts of products. I do not have these tools yet due to the fact that they will certainly be coming out in a number of weeks, once I have them on my hands, I will certainly offer you a quick upgrade.

- **Fill:** The Fill option is primarily to be used for printing as well as patterns. It will only be triggered when you have "Cut" as a "Line Type." Do not fill in forms that you will not print anything. The print is by far, one of the best functions Cricut has due to the fact that it enables you to print your styles, and then cut them; this is remarkable, and also truthfully, it's what motivated me to obtain a Cricut in the first place. When this "Load" alternative is active after you click "Make It;" first, you'll send your data to your home printer and afterward have your Cricut do all the hefty training (cutting.) One more excellent choice for the print kind is patterns. You individuals, this is so trendy. Usage Cricut's options, or publish your own; you can include a pattern to practically any kind of layer. Let's claim it's Valentine's Day, you can make a stunning card with a currently developed pattern from Cricut Access (Subscription, not totally free,) or your own; after that print as well as cut at the same time.

- **Select All:** When you need to relocate all of your components inside the Canvas area, you may have a hard time to select them individually. Click "Select All" to pick all of the elements from the canvas.

- **Edit:** The "Cut" and also "Copy" option will certainly be turned on when you utilize a choice of several elements from the Canvas area. The "Paste" choice will certainly be made it possible when you duplicate or cut something.

- **Align:** If you have previews experience with various other visuals style programs, more than likely you'll recognize just how to utilize this font selection. If you aren't aware of the Align Equipment, let me tell you something; the Align Font selection is something that you intend to understand perfection.

Here's what every Align feature means:

- Align: This function permits you to align all of your layouts, and also it's turned on when picking two or even more elements.

- Line Up Left: When utilizing this setting, all of the aspects will certainly be lined up to the left. The furthest aspect to the left will certainly determine where all of the various other components will certainly move towards.

- Align Right: When using this setting, all of your components will certainly be straightened to the right. The outermost aspect to the right will certainly dictate where all of the various other elements will certainly relocate.

Chapter 5. Cricut Projects For Beginners

If you have just bought your Cricut, you must be pretty eager to get started with some simple DIY designs. The following designs are simple and will help you to manage/work with various materials that can be used with the Cricut machines.

They will also assist you in becoming familiar with some of the tools you will use when creating your designs.

All the projects below assume that you are familiar with Design Space, the materials that can be used with the Cricut, and the various tools you will need for cutting, etc.

Project 1: A Simple Birthday Card

One of the simplest projects to start with is a greeting card. You can use this process to make any type of greeting card you need to make. You can make birthday cards, sympathy cards, milestone cards, and so on.

For this project, we are going to make a birthday card. If you have a milestone birthday coming up, then your Cricut is going to serve you well.

Project Tools, Materials, and Accessories:

- Textured cardstock: light olive-green (or color of your choice).
- Glossy or glitter cardstock: navy blue (or color of your choice).
- Green Standard Grip Cricut mat.
- Cricut Fine-Point Blade.
- Scoring stylus.
- Cricut spatula.
- Pair of scissors for cutting the material to size.
- Glue.

Directions:

1. Login into Design Space and choose "New Project."

2. Once you have logged into Design Space, you will need to choose "Images" from the bar on the left-hand side of the screen.
3. When you are on the "Images" screen, you will need to choose "Cartridges" from the top menu.
4. As you will be making a simple card, in the "Search in Cartridges" box, type in "Simple Cards" as the search criteria. Click the magnifying search button to begin the search.
5. There are 50 images, but only a few will appear on the screen. Click on the "View all 50 images" button next to the box.
6. Scroll through the images until you find the card that reads "Happy Birthday to You." Select the card and insert the image.
7. You will find that this birthday card comes with an envelope design. Highlight the envelope and hide it.
8. Change the size of the card so that it fits into a standard-sized envelope you can get at the store. Change the width to 10" and the height to 7".
9. Now is a good time to save the project. Choose a name you will recognize as you may want to use this project at a later stage. You should remember to save at important stages of the project as you progress through it.
10. Be careful with the stock board when you position it at the top of the mat. It has a tendency to peel back a bit when the

Cricut starts to cut. Position the card mid-way to the bottom of the mat in Design Space.

11. When you put the actual cardstock onto the mat, you must put it with the textured side down. There will be a written message on the inside, which will be the smooth side.
12. In Design Space where you are setting the design, click "Mirror" to flip the card correctly.
13. Select a font you like and type "Happy Birthday" positioned in the center of the card on the right-hand side.
14. You will need to choose "Score" to get a line down the center where you will be folding the card. You do not need to use this, but it is handy. You can just as easily fold the card by hand if you do not have the scoring stylus.
15. After you click "Continue," the next step is to set up the material.
16. As the pattern is quite intricate, use the "Cardstock" (for intricate cuts.) Check your dial to make sure it is set correctly (use the custom setting.)
17. Load the scoring stylus and the fine-point blade. Make sure they are loaded in the Cricut and selected in Design Space.
18. Place the olive-green cardstock on the mat with the rough side down.
19. Position it in the Cricut.
20. Load the mat into the Cricut, and press the "Load/Unload" button.

21. Press the "Go" button when you are ready, and let the machine cut out the card.
22. Once the card has been cut, peel the mat away from the card. Use the spatula to carefully peel the card away, trying not to break the fine cut of the card.
23. Use two-sided tape or glue around the inside of the front of the card.
24. Cut the navy blue glossy or glitter cardstock to match the size of the card. Make it a tiny bit smaller.
25. Glue it or stick it down onto the card.
26. Your card is now ready to use.

Project 2: "Welcome to Our Happy Home" Sign

A nice "Welcome to Our Home Sign" can warm up any entry hall. Choose a nice piece of wood, paint it a happy color, then use your Cricut to make an awesome sign to put on it. Use a chalk finish paint to paint your board, and use a bit of sandpaper to make it a little rough to help the vinyl stick. You can customize the sign to say anything you want, but for this exercise, we are going to use "Welcome to Our Happy Home."

Project Tools, Materials, and Accessories:

- A square wooden board the size you want your sign to be.
- Baby blue paint with a matte or chalk finish (paint the wood before making the sign.)
- Permanent outdoor vinyl (black.)
- Green Standard Grip cutting mat.
- Cricut Fine-Point Blade.
- Pair of scissors for cutting the material to size.
- Weeder tool.
- Spatula.
- Brayer for smoothing out the material.

Directions:

1. Take the measurement of your board the width and length.
2. In Design Space, select "Shapes" from the left-hand menu and choose a square.
3. Resize the square by typing in the dimensions of your board.
4. You will need to zoom the shape in to be able to see it on the screen.

5. You can have the background of the shape in any color. If your text is going to be white, you may want to consider making the box black.
6. Next, you will need to choose a font for the writing on your sign.
7. Click on the "Text" option on the right-hand side menu bar.
8. Type "Welcome to Our Happy Home."
9. Position the text onto the box frame on the screen mimicking where you are going to position the writing on your signboard.
10. For this project, choose Aaron Script single-layer cutting font. It is a nice curly font for a sign.
11. Choose the color you want the writing for your sign to be. For the sake of this exercise, we are going to make the font black.
12. Drag the corner of the text box to size the font to how big you want to make it. It must fit comfortably on your signboard.
13. Remove your template box as you no longer need it and it is not going to be cut.
14. Now is also a good time to save your project and give it a name you will recognize for future similar projects.
15. Make sure you have the correct size cutting board.
16. Cut the vinyl to the size you need. If you have made your fonts to fit completely across your sign, make sure the piece is big enough to fit your signboard.

17. Place the vinyl on the Cricut cutting mat. Here is a tip for you: If your mat is losing its stickiness, you need a bit of tape to anchor it firmly to the mat.
18. In Design Space, click "Make It" in the top right-hand corner of the screen.
19. Set the material to vinyl.
20. You do not need a pen or accessory in the first holder, but you will need to use the fine-point blade in the second holder.
21. Load the cutting board with the vinyl and press the "Load\Unload" button.
22. When the light flashes, the Cricut is loaded and ready to press "Go."
23. Gently peel back the vinyl. You may need to use the spatula to help peel the back vinyl off.
24. Use the weeder tool to hook away any vinyl from the middle of the words, for instance, the V-indent on top of the M. Try not to let any vinyl you have hooked fall back down as it may land crookedly and mess up your letter.
25. Once you have cleaned the vinyl from the words, use the transfer tape and ease it over the letters. Smooth it over the letters as best you can as you pull the back sheet of the transfer tape off. Try not to get bubbles in the tape by using the brayer to smooth the tape out.
26. Once you have the transfer tape on the letters, position it where you want to lay it out on your signboard.

27. If you feel you need guidelines, draw them out with a pencil.
28. Gently peel the white side of the transfer tape from the writing. Then position the top part of the sign where you want to start it on your signboard. Smooth out the rest of the sign.
29. Once the letters are positioned and stuck down with the top part of the transfer tape, give them a rub to ensure they are stuck down.
30. Gently pull the top of the transfer tape off the wording and your sign is ready.

Project 3: "Queen B" T-Shirt

T-Shirts are one of the top items to make with the Cricut, and you will soon find yourself being inundated by friends and family asking you to make them, especially once you have mastered the art and are making extra trendy designs.

For this project, we are going to make a T-Shirt that says "Queen B" with a cute bee hovering over the B.

Project Tools, Materials, and Accessories:

- Plain cotton T-Shirt in the color of your choice.
- Iron-on vinyl also called heat transfer vinyl (HTV)—gold.
- Green Standard Grip mat.
- Cricut Fine-Point Blade.
- Weeding tool.
- Pair of scissors for cutting the material to size.
- Brayer.
- Iron or the Cricut EasyPress Iron.
- Cricut heat press mat to iron on.

Directions:

1. Start a new project in Design Space.
2. Choose "Templates" from the left-hand side menu.
3. Choose the "Classic T-Shirts" template.
4. From the top menu, choose the type of T-Shirt (kids short sleeve.)
5. From the top menu, choose the size of the T-Shirt (small.)
6. The back and the front of the T-Shirt will appear on Design Space in the workspace.

7. From the top menu, select the color of the T-Shirt you are using (pink).
8. Select "Text" from the left-hand menu and type in "Queen B."
9. Set the font; a great free font for this project is Bauhaus 93.
10. Position the text on the T-Shirt, then set the size and change the color to gold.
11. Choose images and find a bee picture. There is a nice free image or some really cute images you can buy.
12. Position the bee above the B and set the color to gold. You can rotate it into a tilted position.
13. Click on the "Make It' button, and you will be prompted with another screen showing the design on the cutting board. This is because, for iron-on vinyl, you need to mirror the image. You mirror the image in order to iron it on with the correct side up. Click the "Mirror" button on the left-hand side of the screen. You will see your writing and image look like it is back-to-front. You may want to move the bee over a bit giving a bit of space between the image and writing.
14. Reset your dial on the Cricut to custom.
15. In Design Space, choose the everyday iron-on for your material setting.
16. You can set the pressure to a bit more if you like.
17. You will see a warning letting you know that mirroring must be on for iron-on vinyl. It reminds you to place the vinyl facedown as well.

18. Check that you have the fine-point blade loaded in cartridge two of the Cricut. Nothing is needed for cartridge one.
19. Cut the vinyl to the space that is indicated by the Cricut Design Space.
20. Place the shiny side of the iron-on vinyl down onto the cutting mat. Use your brayer to smooth out the vinyl onto your mat.
21. Load the cutting into the Cricut, and when the Cricut is ready, click "Go" for it to cut.
22. Unload the cutting mat when it has been cut. Remove the design from the mat, and gently remove the mat side of the vinyl from the carrier sheet (matte side of the vinyl.)
23. Use the weeding tool to pick out the areas of the letters like the middles of the B.
24. Place your T-Shirt onto the Cricut pressing mat with the middle section where you want the transfer to be.
25. If you are using the Cricut EasyPress, you can go to the Cricut website to find the heat transfer guide and the settings you will need for the press. Follow the instructions with the Cricut EasyPress.
26. For a normal iron, preheat the iron.
27. Place the Cricut heat press mat inside the shirt.
28. Heat the surface of the T-Shirt for 15 seconds with the iron.
29. Put the design on the shirt where it is to be ironed on with the carrier sheet up.

30. Place a parchment sheet over the vinyl to protect the iron and the design.
31. Place the iron on the design and hold the iron in place on the design applying a bit of pressure for up to 30 seconds.
32. Turn the shirt inside out and place the iron on the back of the design for another 30 seconds.
33. When it is done, turn the shirt right side out and gently pull the carrier sheet off.
34. Don't wash the shirt for 24 hours after the transfer has been done.

Project 4: Personalized Paper Bookmark

Make a personalized paper bookmark for textbooks and reading books.

Project Tools, Materials, and Accessories:

- Cardstock 8 ½" by 11" (color and type of your choice.)
- Green Standard Grip mat.
- Cricut Fine-Point Blade.
- Weeding tool.
- Spatula.
- Pair of scissors for cutting the material to size.

Directions:

1. Create a new project in Design Space.
2. Choose "Shapes" and select the square.
3. Unlock the square by clicking on the little lock at the bottom left-hand corner of the square.
4. With the square selected, change the shape to 6" wide and 2" high.
5. With the square still selected, click on "Duplicate" in the box on the right-hand side.
6. Select the copy you have made of the rectangle, unlock it, and set the width to 5.5" by 1.5" height.
7. Move the smaller box into the middle of the larger box.
8. Select both of the shapes and click on "Slice" at the bottom right-hand corner of the screen.
9. Remove the box in the middle of the rectangle and delete it.

10. In the middle of the larger box, you will see another smaller rectangular shape. Select it, move it out of the larger box, and delete it.
11. Select text from the left-hand menu. Choose a font. A good one for this is Bauhaus 93 or Cooper Black.
12. Type the name for the bookmark (Chloe.)
13. Move the name to the middle of the rectangle box, centering it, and then stretching it so it fills the hollow middle of the rectangle.
14. Select the rectangle and the name, click on "Copy," and make another three. You can make around four to five bookmarks on an 8 ½" by 11" cardstock.
15. Change the names on the other three bookmarks. Highlight each one separately and then click on "Weld" in the bottom right-hand corner (this must be done to each bookmark separately.)
16. Save your project.
17. Place your cardstock onto the cutting mat and load it into the Cricut.
18. Click "Make It" in Design Space.
19. Select the materials, which will be the cardstock you have chosen.
20. Check that all the cartridges are loaded in the Cricut and you have the fine-point blade loaded.
21. When the Cricut flashes ready, press "Go" to cut out your cards.

22. When the printing is finished, remove the cardstock from the cutting mat, and use the spatula to ensure it comes off without ruining the cut.
23. Clean up the letters with the weeding tool.
24. Your bookmarks are ready for use

Project 5: Fancy Leather Bookmark

Personalized leather bookmarks make really nice gifts. They are also very easy to make with the Cricut.

Project Tools, Materials, and Accessories:

- Cricut metallic leather.
- Cricut holographic iron-on (red for a gold effect.)
- Purple StrongGrip mat.

- Cricut Fine-Point Blade.
- Weeding tool.
- Pair of scissors for cutting the material to size.
- Brayer or scraping tool.
- Cricut Knife Blade.
- Thin gold string or ribbon.

Directions:

1. Cut the leather to the size you want it to be.
2. Each leather holder is approximately 2" wide by 6" high.
3. Cut the holographic paper to the size you want it to be; this will depend on the size of the font and wording you choose for the bookmark.
4. Create a new project in Design Space.
5. Select "Shapes" from the left-hand menu.
6. Choose the square, unlock it, and set the width to 2" with a height of 6".
7. Choose a triangle from the "Shapes" menu, and set the width to 1.982" and the height to 1.931".
8. Position the triangle in the rectangle at the bottom. Make sure it is positioned evenly as this is going to create a swallowtail for the bookmark.
9. Select the circle from the shapes menu, and unlock the shape. Set the width and height to 0.181".

10. Duplicate the circle shape.
11. Move one circle to the top right-hand corner of the bookmark and the other to the left. These will be the holes to put a piece of ribbon or fancy string through.
12. Align the holes and distribute them evenly by using the "Align" function from the top menu with both circles selected.
13. Select the top left hole with the top of the rectangle and click "Slice" in the bottom right menu.
14. Select the circle and remove it, then delete it.
15. Select the top right circle with the top of the rectangle and click "Slice" from the bottom right menu.
16. Select the circle and remove it.
17. Select the bookmark and move it over until you see the other two circles.
18. Select the two circles and delete them.
19. Select the triangle and the bottom of the rectangle, then click "Slice" from the bottom right-hand menu.
20. Select the first triangle, remove it, and delete it.
21. Select the second triangle, remove it, and delete it.
22. Save your project.
23. You will now have the first part of your leather bookmark ready to print.
24. Place the leather on the cutting mat, and use the brayer tool or scraper tool to flatten it and stick it properly to the cutting mat.

25. Position the little rollers on the feeding bar to the left and right so they do not run over the leather.
26. Set the dial on the Cricut to custom.
27. Load the knife blade into the second Cricut chamber.
28. In Design Space, click on "Make It."
29. Set the material to Cricut metallic leather.
30. Load the cutting board and leather into the Cricut and hit "Go" when the Cricut is ready to cut.
31. Unload the cutting board when the Cricut is finished printing and use the spatula to cut the leather bookmark form out.
32. Use the weeding tool to remove any shapes that should not be on the bookmark.
33. Place the holographic paper on the cutting mat, and put the wheels on the loading bar back into their position.
34. Create a new project in Design Space, and choose a nice fancy font. Do not make it any bigger than 1.5" wide and 3" high.
35. Save the project.
36. Click on "Make It," and choose the correct material.
37. Mirror the image.
38. Switch the blade in the second chamber back to the fine-point blade.
39. Load the cutting board and click "Go" when the Cricut is ready to cut.

40. Gently peel the back off the design, heat the leather, and place the name on the bookmark where you want it positioned.
41. Use the same iron-on method as the method in the "Queen B" T-Shirt project above.
42. Your bookmark is now ready to use or give as a personalized gift.

Project 6: Personalized Envelopes

Making personalized envelopes for those personalized greeting cards adds that extra touch.

Project Tools, Materials, and Accessories:

- Envelope 5.5" by 4.25".
- Cricut pens in the color of your choice.
- Green Standard Grip mat.
- Spatula.

Directions:

1. Create a new project in Design Space.
2. Choose the square from the "Shapes" menu.
3. Unlock the square, set the width to 5.5" and the height to 4.25".
4. Choose "Text" from the right-hand menu.
5. This will be the name and address the envelope will be addressed to.
6. Choose a font and size it to fit comfortably in the middle of the envelope.
7. You can choose a different color for the font.
8. Move the text box to the middle of the envelope.
9. Select the entire envelope and click "Attach" from the bottom right-hand menu.
10. When you move the card around the screen, the address text will move with the envelope.
11. Load the envelope onto the cutting board and load it into the Cricut.
12. In Design Space, click "Make It."

13. Choose a material like paper.
14. Check to see if the pen color you need is loaded into the first compartment of the Cricut.
15. When the project is ready, press "Go" and let it print.
16. Flip the card over and stick it onto the mat.
17. Use a piece of tape to stick the envelope flap down.
18. Load it into the Cricut.
19. Change the text on the envelope to a return address or "Regards From."
20. Change the color of the pen if you want the writing in another color.
21. When you are ready, click on "Make It."
22. Make sure the material is set to the correct setting.
23. When you are ready, press "Go."

24. Once it has finished cutting, you will have a personalized envelope.

Chapter 6. Making Money With Cricut

Just as the Cricut machine can be used in a million and one ways (figuratively speaking,) the ways to generate money from it is also numerous.

Some of the ways to generate money from the Cricut machine are highlighted below:

Make and Sell Leather Bracelets

Bracelets are fashionable items, especially leather bracelet. The Cricut machine can easily cut real or faux leather easily giving you less work to do. If you decide to cut, make, and sell leather bracelets, know that the materials needed are just snaps: your Cricut machine, leather, and probably card stock.

If you are interested in selling this craft, you can also create room for preordering, where a buyer can order for a particular design to be created by the designer.

Sell Iron-On Vinyl

This is another money-making opportunity that the Cricut machine provides. You make a design with the iron-on vinyl and sell out to people. The iron-on vinyl can be in the form of text or design. It can also be made for each season or celebration, be it Valentine, Halloween, Christmas, or Easter. Buyers may also order for what they want.

Sell Stickers

This idea is targeted at kids. You can make money by designing educative and entertaining stickers for toddlers and other age groups. Stickers of the alphabet, or map of a locale can be made. Stickers are also used in decorating places like the wardrobe or closets.

Make and Sell Party Decorations and Buntings

There is always a celebration in our day-to-day lives as human beings. It can be a milestone celebration, or simply a fun-seeking escapade. Party decorations made with the Cricut machine can be sold on these occasions.

Other Ideas To Explore

The following are other income generating ideas with the Cricut machine:

Window Decals: Everyone has a peculiar image, an object we are practically obsessed with. Getting a vinyl window decal of one's favorite image will go a long way in giving your decor a boost. Making and selling window decals is quite easy and profitable.

Make and Sell Canvas Wall Art: Customized wall art would generate quick and easy money. Get inspirational sayings or designs, and make them into wall arts for sale.

Design and Sell Onesies: Onesies or bodysuit are generally cute cloth which can be better with amazing artwork. Onesies for babies can be made with a lot of other text apart from "Daddy loves you" or "Momma's baby." Other mushy word art can be used in designing onesies for kids.

Become a Cricut Affiliate: This entails being paid to make tutorials video by the Cricut company. These videos are uploaded to the internet for the netizen to make use of. To become a Cricut affiliate, you need to have a strong internet presence. You must also have a tangible amount of followers on your social media accounts.

Post Tutorial Videos on Your Vlog: This has nothing to do with being an affiliate; rather, you create a blog for videos and upload tutorial videos, and get paid through the generated traffic.

Use of Social Media: You can make any of the craft you find easy and post pictures of it online, announcing to those on your list that it is for sale. This works better because whoever is buying gets to see the picture of whatever he is getting before ordering for it. Personalized crafts should also be included in your order of business.

Design and Sell T-Shirts: A T-Shirt is a clothing piece that is always in vogue. Most especially for college students, a designed tee would be a great fashion item. Creating a designed T-Shirt would generate income.

Design and Sell Hoodies: Hoodies are great wear for cold seasons. A designed one would roll better with the youth. The design can be preordered too.

Design and Sell Leather Neck Piece: A leather pendant can be designed for a necklace and sold out to interested buyers. An all-leather neck piece can also be made and sold.

Design and Sell Banners: Banners can be made for celebrations, festive periods, camping, parties, religious activities, or sporting activities. All these can be made and sold.

Design and Sell Window Clings: Window clings with the design of the seasons can be made and sold. Other designs or images can also be used for creating window clings.

Design and Sell Stencils: Stencils can be created and sold for those that want to hand-paint a post or sign. It would also generate a nice amount of money.

Design and sell safari animal Stickers: Stickers of safari animals are attractive items. They can be made and sold to animal lovers. The sticker is easy to make, and will also be a source of income generation.

Design and Sell Labeling Stickers: Labeling stickers can be made for labeling things in the house. Things in the kitchen, pantry, playroom, classroom, and other places can be labeled with labeling stickers.

Design and Sell Labeling Vinyl: Labeling adhesive vinyl can be made for labeling things in the house. Things in the kitchen, pantry, playroom, classroom, and other places can be labeled with labeling vinyl.

Design and Cut Appliqués: Fancy fabrics can be made into appliqués to design or decorate a place or object.

Design and Sell Christmas Ornaments: Christmas is a period when people celebrate and decorate their workplace, abode, and religious settings, among others.

Design and Sell Wall Decals: Different designs of wall decals can be made and sold for a cheap and affordable price.

Design and Sell Doormats: Beautiful doormat can be made with the machine and sold to customers. It can be designed with either text or images. Customized doormats can also be sold.

Design and Sell Kitchen Towels: Towels used in the kitchen can be designed and sold at affordable prices. The towels can be designed with text or images of delicacies.

Conclusion: Tips For Start In The Best Way

There are a lot of things which you can achieve by making the correct use of your machine. However, it is not just enough to know these, you need to know easier and more improved ways to make use of the machine you have acquired. To make the most out of your newly-acquired machine, here are a few things you should do:

1. **Test out your machine first.** This is a no-brainer, and you should do it as soon as the machine arrives. It is always a safe idea to start by testing out the components of your machine and double-checking to ensure that your machine has all the accessories that were promised. If at this stage, you discover that your machine is missing a few things, you may want to reach out to membership support immediately and get the issues rectified.

2. **Keep the components of your machine (especially the cutting mat) clean.** This is one of the parts of the machine that is constantly subjected to wear, tear, attack by dirt, and spoiling. In order to make sure that your machine

remains in the best of conditions, take out time to clean your mat frequently. Best practices when you are trying to get this done is to make use of a lint roller to wipe down the mat after every use and to also scan over the mat once you are done with it to make sure that you take out all the little pieces that may remain from the materials you just cut. Also, be sure to frequently replace the plastic protective sheet that came with the mat, and it is not entirely unheard for you to wash the mat frequently too. However, washing the mat can be a tricky business. Considering the fact that the mat is meant to be in a specific way, you need to make sure that you wash it in such a way that you do not compromise the integrity of the material the mat is made of. For best practices, wash with lukewarm water and mild dish soap. With these, scrub gently in circular patterns, rinse and allow the mat to drip dry.

3. **Cutting certain materials require that your mat be a bit sticky so that it can hold the material you are looking to cut in place.** Due to some factors like prolonged use, and continuous subjection to heavy work, there may be times that you would need to cut something that requires that the mat has a firm grip on the material, but you may not have access to a good mat that has not lost its stickiness at that time. As a way around this, you can resort to using masking tape or painter's tape to hold the

material you are looking to cut in place. However, take this as a cue to change mats because this option won't work forever.

4. **In order to prevent the confusion that can come as a result of having to deal with many blades that you will need for your different projects, it can be safe to adopt the pattern of storing up your blades in such a way that you can tell almost instantly what blade is used to cut what material.** In essence, it is vital for you to learn to separate your blades. Let there be blades that you use to cut vinyl, then the ones you use to cut paper, and wood, and all the rest of them. This will ensure that your blades last for much longer and that you don't use the wrong blades for the wrong projects, thereby creating troubles for your new machine. You can get started by finding small jars to hold the blades, and then labeling each jar to signify which blades go into it. This way, you do not run the risk of making a mistake with your blade placement.

5. **You do not always have to have the right color of vinyl for you to embark upon your projects.** Let's assume that you are about to get started with a project and you need some green vinyl, but all you have is pink-colored vinyl, you must not get dressed and go off to the mall to get the green-colored ones because there is a way around it.

Instead of running off to the mall every time you need a different color of vinyl, why not get some Rustoleum Metallic Spray paint for the future. With this, you can give your un-cut vinyl some spraying and color-over without having to spend money every time. Just for a few bucks, you can get this over with.

6. **Dafont.com and 1001freefonts.com are amazing websites where you can find tons of fonts that you can make use of to create even more epic designs.** If you have searched through the Design Space and you have not been able to see something that piques your interests, or you just need to try out something new, you may want to visit those platforms and see what they have in store for you. Also, you will find a lot of support groups on Facebook where you can find a lot of helpful information as regards your creative journey with the machine you have just acquired. Join these groups, and be sure to be an active member of them. You will see that there are some things that may bother you that can be a walkover for another person. All you need to do is reach out. Furthermore, these platforms serve as hosting sites for a ton of helpful tools that can even unclog your creativity even more. Find them as pinned documents, helpful DIY tips, post and comment threads, and in all other formats as they come. The goal is to make sure that you do not try to do this on your own.

7. **Want to do some stenciling, but you are not sure where and how you can get started?** There's no need for you to be confused when you can make use of freezer paper to create custom stencils for your projects. With the Cricut Explore Air 2, you can get to cut the paper and fashion it into some custom-design stencils for your projects.

8. **Make use of tin foils to sharpen your blades.** Notwithstanding how careful you are with the blades, and how you do not mistake them for cutting different materials, it is not possible for your blades not to get to a point where they become blunt and weak. When your blades get blunt, a great way to get them up and running once again is by making use of tin foils to sharpen them. By sharpening with tin foil, you can extend the life of your blade, almost by x3. Sharpening is very simple. All you need to do is to unclamp the blade and run the tip of the blade through the tin foil between 10-15 times.

9. **Using pens other than the Cricut pens to write.** Next to the Cricut pens, there are a ton of other brands that you can make use of, even with your machine. They include:

    - Uni-ball Signo UM-153.

    - Tombow Dual brush pens.

- Sakura gelly roll.

- Bic marking and Bic crystal.

- Pilot precise.

The list is basically endless. The best part is that for all these pens, you can find them online, and with just a few dollars, you can have them added to your bucket list of pens to work with. However, to make use of these pens with your machine, you need a pen adapter. Pen adapters work for the Explore Air 2, or newer models of the Cricut machine. With these, you can connect any brand of Cricut pens and draw/write away.

10. **Increase your image options by learning how to make your own SVG files online.** While the Design Space and the internet provide you with endless numbers of images, you will agree that there are those times when even the most intricately designed picture does not quite cut it; it does not do justice to what you want to create. Under these circumstances, you need to learn how to bring your inner genius to life.

Using Inkscape, you can create your own SVG files from scratch, or convert your boring pictures to two-layered SVG files. Inkscape is a free tool that you can make use of, and making use of it is relatively easy.

11. **The following step is to make the best use of all the craft creation related wisdom in the context of Cricut cutting machines to embark on your own creative journey and make a whole lot of money while doing so.** You are now equipped with all the tools and understanding required to create your own unique craft projects that will serve as a medium to channel your creativity. All the Cricut devices are uniquely designed to help you create real-life crafts stemming even from the most unlikely to manifest craft ideas. The results are professional looking with a high finish that you can not only use for your home décor but potentially sell to others with a similar creative wavelength. To help you accomplish this, all the nuances of the Design Space application have been explained in exquisite detail, along with information on a variety of free design resources such as images, fonts, and projects. This guidebook has utilized and presented a variety of beginner-friendly projects that can be accessed through the Cricut library on the Design Space application, so you can enhance your craft skills or learn to be a craftsman without heavily investing in machines and tools.

www.ingramcontent.com/pod-product-compliance
Lightning Source LLC
Chambersburg PA
CBHW071517080526
44588CB00011B/1455